Creative Christmas

Handmade Decorations and Gifts

CREATIVE
HOME
ARTS
CLUB—

MINNETONKA,
MINNESOTA

Creative Home
Arts Library™

Creative Christmas
Handmade Decorations and Gifts

Printed in 2007.

Tom Carpenter
Creative Director

Jen Weaverling
Production Editor

Julie Cisler
Senior Graphic Designer

Phil Aarrestad
Principal Photographer

Contributing Writers
Sue Banker
Jana Freiband
Zoe Graul
Teresa Henn
MaryBeth Kissling
Margaret Hanson-Maddox
Lorine Mason
Nancy Maurer
Cheryl Natt
Cheryl Nelson

Special thanks to: Terry Casey, Janice Cauley, Alison Brown Cerier, Bob Green, Heather Koshiol, Happi Olson, Maggie Stopera and Susan Telleen.

2 3 4 5 6 7 8 9 10 / 12 11 10 09 08 07
© 2006 Creative Home Arts Club
ISBN 10: 1-58159-287-6
ISBN 13: 978-1-58159-287-0

Creative Home Arts Club
12301 Whitewater Drive
Minnetonka, MN 55343
www.creativehomeartsclub.com

Contents

Introduction

Christmas is a time of celebration. Add to the warmth, glow and good cheer of the season with festive, handmade creations from *Creative Christmas*. Here are dozens upon dozens of *Handmade Decorations and Gifts* ... great ideas to inspire you, along with step-by-step instructions, making it easy for you to create these delightful holiday accessories.

**Page 120
Message Board
and Magnets**

**Page 46
Snowman Jester Stick**

Whether it's around your home, under your tree or on your tabletop, *Creative Christmas* offers endless opportunities to celebrate the season. With projects for trimming the tree, decking the halls, setting the table, giving gifts and adding finishing touches, *Creative Christmas* will guide you to your most beautiful and festive Christmas yet.

A lovely full-color photo starts each project, displaying the finished creation so you know what you're working toward. Lists of materials and tools outline what you need to complete the project. Full-color photos guide you through each project to assure your success and satisfaction.

It's time to get a *Creative Christmas* pulled together in your home. The rewards will be breathtaking indeed. Go ahead and get started, and celebrate with your own creations!

CREATIVE
HOME
ARTS
—CLUB—

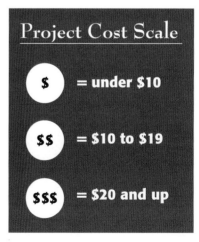

Project Cost Scale

$ = under $10

$$ = $10 to $19

$$$ = $20 and up

5

Chapter 1

Trim the Tree

Confetti Tree Skirt

A sprinkling of buttons and a feather boa make a playful skirt for a mini-tree. For a full-size version, cut a felt circle the desired size and use the biggest buttons you can find. Boas are sold in craft and toy stores.

Materials

- ³/₄ yard white felt
- Fabric marker
- Red embroidery floss
- Assorted bright buttons, tiny to 1¹/₄-inch diameter
- 75-inch red feather boa

Tools

- Straightedge
- Scissors

1 Fold felt in half. Fold again with the folded side together and edges even.

2 Measure 12 inches from folded tip and mark. Tie fabric marker to length of floss or string. Hold marker upright at the mark. With your other hand, press other end of floss at folded tip of felt. Draw arc. Cut all layers together. Unfold. Cut line from edge to center of circle. Cut three crossing slits at center for tree trunk.

3 Sew buttons randomly across the felt, singly or in layers, knotting all but the smallest on top. To make knots that show on a two-hole button, insert the threaded needle through a button hole on the button front and then through the felt. Pull the floss to the back leaving a 2-inch tail. Bring needle up through the remaining hole; knot floss ends. For a four-hole button, insert the needle through a button hole on the front and then through the felt. Pull the floss to the back leaving a 2-inch tail. Bring needle up through an adjacent hole. Push the needle down through the opposite hole and up through the remaining hole; knot and trim ends.

4 Using long stitches from back of skirt, tack feather boa around edge.

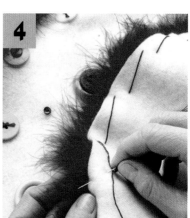

Jolly Ribbon Rounds

You'll be decking the halls in no time with these easy ornaments. Just snip squares of grosgrain ribbon and pin them to a foam ball.

Materials

- 3-inch Styrofoam ball
- 3 to 4 yards grosgrain ribbon in a variety of widths, colors, and patterns
- Pins with color-ball heads

3 Cut about 40 squares from a variety of ribbons. Pin squares on ornament to cover. Arrange squares in even rows or randomly.

Tools

- Pencil
- Scissors

1 Poke hole in ball with the pencil.

2 Cut 10-inch piece of ribbon. Pin both ends of ribbon into hole to form a hanger for the ornament.

Candyland Garland

Decorate evergreens
with this playful garland
of beads and sweets.

$$

12

Materials for a 12-Foot Garland

- 48 (9/16-inch) round wood beads
- 12 (1½-inch) wood toy wheels
- 24 (¾-inch) wood spools
- 12 (1-inch) round wood beads
- 8 feet red wood bead garland
- Acrylic craft paints: light blue, bright pink, purple, crimson, medium orange, medium yellow
- White glitter
- Plastic bags
- White embroidery floss

Tools

- Pencils or dowels
- Small, flat brush
- Thin brush
- Disposable bowl
- Styrofoam block
- Scissors
- Embroidery needle

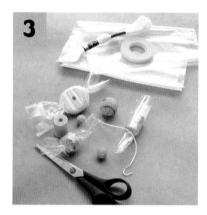

1 Place each wood piece on sharp end of pencil or dowel. Paint small round beads orange, wheels yellow, and spools blue and purple. Insert a pencil into Styrofoam block and allow to dry.

2 Paint 1-inch beads pink. While paint is still wet, paint a winding swirl by twisting the pencil or dowel that holds the ball. Hold the wet bead over the disposable bowl and sprinkle with glitter. Insert the pencil or dowel into the Styrofoam block and allow to dry.

3 Cut 4- by 4-inch squares from the plastic bags. Cut enough 6-inch pieces of floss to wrap the pink beads and the spools. Wrap with holes to sides and secure with floss. Trim tails. Cut enough 5- by 5-inch squares to wrap the wheels. Wrap the wheels flat, and secure with floss.

4 Cut off end of bead garland and remove beads. Thread needle with the thread of the garland. String beads and "candies," putting five beads from the garland between each element. Knot last bead in place.

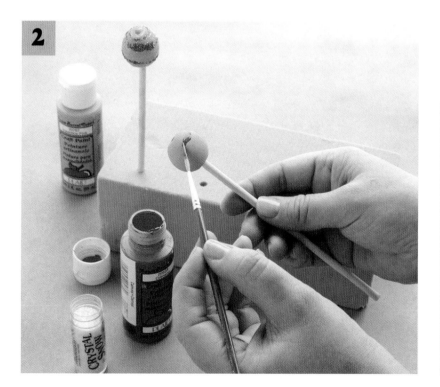

Warm Wishes

Stitch up argyle mittens and trim your tree with warmth. These toddler-sized treasures also make wonderful wrappings for gift cards and holiday cash.

$

14

Materials

- Felt squares, three colors
- Embroidery floss
- Two buttons

Tools

- Fabric marker
- Scissors
- Pins
- Embroidery needle
- Fiberfill (optional)

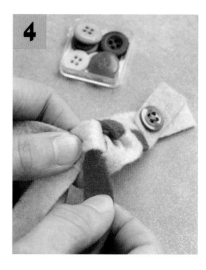

1 Enlarge mitten pattern by 200%. Cut out. Pin to felt and trace. From main color, cut mitten front and back. Trace diamond pattern. From contrasting colors, cut three diamond shapes.

2 Pin diamonds down front of mitten. Sew diamonds with long stitches with an argyle pattern as shown.

3 Leaving cuff open, blanket stitch front and back together.

4 Cut a ⅝- by 10-inch strip of each felt. Stack strips. Sew button 1 inch from the end. Braid strips. When long enough to circle the top of the mitten, sew second button on end. Trim. Hand stitch cuff in place.

5 Cut ½- by 3-inch strip felt. Sew between buttons, forming hanging loop. Stuff mitten with a small amount of fiberfill, or insert a gift card, cash, or tiny gift.

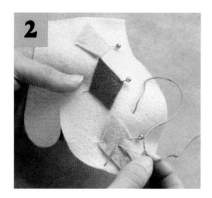

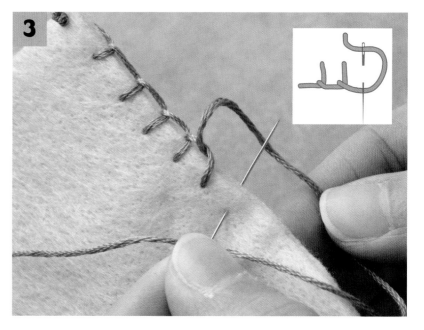

15

Grapevine Star Tree Topper

Make this natural-looking star for the top of your tree. Or hang it on your front door! Copper wire twisted into tendrils decorates the star's points. You can also make this star from willow, which can be purchased in bundles from the craft store.

$

Materials

- 6 to 7 yards grapevine
- 15 small rubber bands
- 4 feet (20-gauge) copper wire
- 2 feet (24-gauge) copper wire
- Ten 10- to 12-mm beads

Tools

- Pruning shears
- Wire cutters
- Scissors
- Needle-nose pliers

1 Using pruning shears, cut grapevine into 14- to 16-inch pieces. Create five bundles of two or three pieces. Wrap rubber band about 1 inch from the ends of each bundle.

2 Arrange bundles in star shape. First create the top point, and bind with rubber band. Next attach one bundle across. Finally, attach the other two bundles. Even up the points, or leave uneven for a folk look.

3 Cut thicker wire into 6-inch pieces. Secure each outer point with a twist of wire, leaving tails long on the front side of the star. Cut thinner wire into 4-inch pieces. Twist one around each inner connecting point. Using the scissors, cut off all the rubber bands.

4 To make a holder, cut two pieces thicker wire twice the width of star. Attach in two places on star, forming loops just big enough for the top of the tree to pass through.

5 Wrapping around the pliers, curl wires at corners of star, leaving last inch straight. Place bead on end of wire and bend wire to hold. Arrange tendrils.

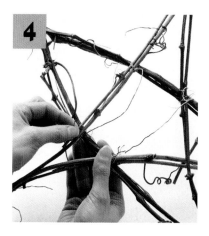

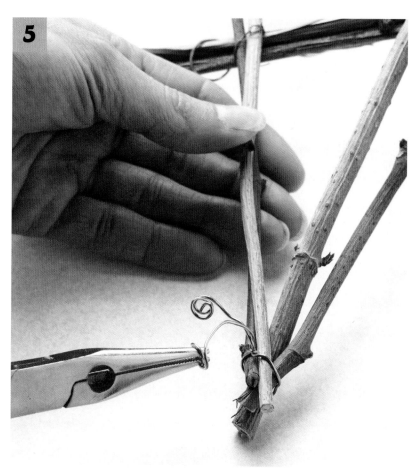

17

Mr. and Mrs. Snowman Ornaments

Create the heads of snow people from paper clay and make them come alive with paint and embellishments. Then decorate your tree, or glue on a pin back to make a lapel pin.

$$

Materials

- Paper clay
- Acrylic craft paints: white, black, orange
- Black permanent marker
- Powdered blusher
- Decoupage medium
- Clear acrylic spray
- Craft glue
- Few beads
- Bit of ribbon
- Craft hair
- Adhesive-backed felt or foam
- 12 inches of No. 30 or No. 20 wire

Tools

- Brush
- Scissors
- Toothpick
- Wire cutters
- Needle-nose pliers

1 Shape paper clay into two heads, a top hat, noses, and any other decorative pieces you would like. Allow to air dry, following package directions.

2 Paint heads white, noses orange, and hat black. Allow to dry.

3 Draw faces with permanent marker. Rub rouge on cheek area. Paint all pieces with decoupage medium. Allow to dry. Spray with clear acrylic spray. Allow to dry.

4 Glue pieces to heads, applying to small pieces with toothpick. Glue hair to Mrs. Snowman's head and glue top hat on Mr. Snowman. Add a bead necklace and a bit of ribbon. Place heads face up on back of adhesive-backed felt or foam. Trace shape and cut out. Attach to backs of heads. Trim if necessary.

5 To form ornament hangers, cut two 6-inch pieces of wire. Curl one end of each with needle-nose pliers. Glue a wire to back of each head. Place permanent adhesive on the wire. Slip wire between the ornament and the felt backing and press felt backing back in place.

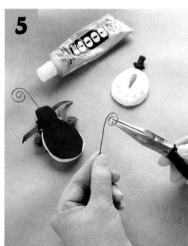

Crazy Block Tree Skirt

These easy pieced blocks create a fun and colorful skirt for a tabletop tree. The finished size is 30 by 30 inches.

Materials

- ¹/₈ yard each of five cotton holiday prints, mix of light and dark
- 1¹/₂ yards solid coordinating fabric
- 1 yard cotton batting
- Thread
- Sixteen jingle bells or buttons

Tools

- Rotary cutter and mat
- See-through ruler
- Yardstick
- Fabric marker
- Scissors
- Pins
- Iron and ironing board
- Sewing machine
- Compass, or dish 4 inches in diameter
- Hand sewing needle

1 Fold two pieces printed fabric in half and stack. Place the ruler near left edge. Make marks 1 inch from top, 1¹/₂ inches further down, and 2 inches further. On right side of the fabric stack, make marks at 2 inches from the top, then 1 inch further, then 1¹/₂ inches. Using yardstick, connect marks across fabric with three lines. Cut. Repeat with other three prints.

2 Line up strips, arranging pieces in the same order they were cut, but varying the prints and alternating lights and darks. Sew strips together with ¹/₄-inch seam allowance. Press all seams in the same direction.

3 Using rotary cutter and ruler, cut pieced fabric into four 6¹/₂-inch strips. Stack two strips together and cut them into 6¹/₂-inch squares. You will have 12 crazy blocks.

4 Using rotary cutter and ruler, cut 13 blocks of solid fabric, each 6¹/₂ inches square.

5 Arrange blocks into five rows of five blocks. Start first row with solid, and alternate solid and pieced blocks. Sew one row of blocks together, with a ¹/₄-inch seam allowance. Press seams toward solid squares. Repeat with all rows. Pin the rows together and sew. Press.

6 Cut solid fabric and batting the same size as the pieced fabric. Stack with batting on bottom, then plain fabric right-side up, then pieced fabric right-side down. Pin together along edges. Using compass, trace 4-inch circle in center square. Mark

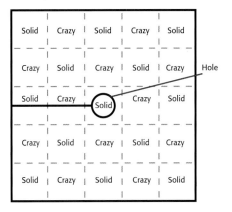

Solid	Crazy	Solid	Crazy	Solid
Crazy	Solid	Crazy	Solid	Crazy
Solid	Crazy	Solid	Crazy	Solid
Crazy	Solid	Crazy	Solid	Crazy
Solid	Crazy	Solid	Crazy	Solid

Hole

line from circle's center to center of one edge of skirt. Pin near markings and cut. Stitch tree skirt together, using a ¹/₄-inch seam allowance, leaving an opening. Trim corners. Turn right side out, poking out corners. Press. Press seam allowance under at opening and slipstitch closed.

7 Hand stitch a bell or button at each intersection.

Winter Fun Ornaments

These ornaments capture the fun of winter sports! The instructions are for one ornament, but you can easily make a half-dozen at a time. Create a theme tree!

Materials

- Polymer clay: granite blue, silver
- Two 3- by 4-inch pieces of white felt
- Blue embroidery floss
- ¹/₂-inch sparkle pom-poms
- 9-mm silver jingle bells
- Narrow ribbons
- Child's striped tights
- Thread

Tools

- Baking sheet
- Oven
- Tracing paper
- Fabric marker
- Embroidery needle
- Newspaper
- Waxed paper
- Rolling pin
- Craft knife
- Straightedge
- Paper clip
- Sewing needle
- Hot glue gun and glue stick

1 To make each skate ornament, roll silver polymer clay into two ropes 6 inches long and size of a pipe cleaner. Shape into long ovals. Put on sheet and bake according to package directions. Allow to cool. Enlarge skate pattern to 135% and cut out. Pin to white felt. Cut two skate pieces. Using a doubled strand of embroidery floss, stitch three X's up the front of the skate, ending with threads on top. String a pom-pom on each floss end, knot approximately 1¹/₂ inches from the felt and trim the tails. Hand stitch skate pieces together with long running stitches, catching blade and sewing a jingle bell to the toe. Sew hanging loop at top.

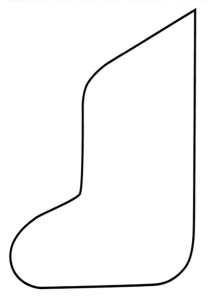

2 To make a set of skis, first cover work surface with several layers of newspaper and piece waxed paper. Roll blue clay to ¹/₈ inch thick. Using craft knife and straightedge, cut two strips ³/₈ inch by 4 inches. Trim one end into point and curve up the ski. Flatten the silver clay. Cut four ³/₈- by ⁷/₈-inch pieces.

Press one rectangle on each ski piece, pressing at each end with paper clip. Bake. Allow to cool. Cross the skis just behind the silver pieces and glue. Tie ribbons where skis cross.

3 To make a hat, cut a 3¹/₂-inch length from tights. Roll one end to form a brim. Gather the opposite end with running stitches; pull tight and knot. Glue pom-pom to top.

Contemporary Cone Ornament

The Victorians made cone ornaments from printed papers. This contemporary version is bigger and brighter. Place it on your tree or mantel and fill with candy, colorful tissue paper or other bright and festive goodies.

$

Materials

- Three squares felt: lime green, red, coordinating print
- Two sheets paper
- Heavy paper
- Tape
- Thread
- Green and red cotton yarn
- Fabric glue
- Clothespins

Tools

- Compass
- Scissors
- Straightedge
- Sewing machine
- Hole punch

1 Make the basic pattern by placing point of compass in corner of a sheet of paper; trace a 6-inch quarter circle; cut out. To make wedge pattern, fold basic pattern in thirds along the curve; trace onto paper; add 1 inch to each straight side for fringe and cut out. To make lining pattern, place basic pattern on paper and trace, adding 1 1/4 inches on the curved edge; cut out.

2 Place basic pattern on heavy paper and trace around. Cut out. Roll a cone shape with edges touching but not overlapping. Secure with tape.

3 Place wedge pattern on a piece of print felt and trace. Cut out. Repeat for the other two pieces of felt. Pin wedges together. Sew 1 inch from the edges. Cut fringe about 1/2 inch wide and just short of the stitching.

4 Place paper cone into felt cone, trimming paper if necessary. Attach with few dabs of glue at the top.

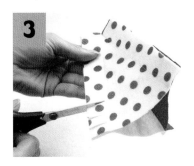

5 Place lining pattern on solid felt and trace. Cut. Roll felt lining into cone shape and place in paper cone. Glue together sparingly. Cut fringe along top of lining. Place cone upside down to bend fringe evenly while drying.

6 To make hanger, punch two holes on opposite sides of the cone and 1/2 inch from the top. Twist yarns together. Thread through holes from the inside out and knot. Add dots of glue toward the base of fringe and fold fringe down, holding with clothespins until glue is dry.

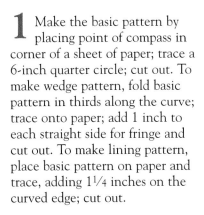

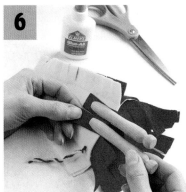

Cherished Picture Ornament

This is a perfect gift for any parent or grandparent. Add new photos as new children or grandchildren come along, or to show how much a child has grown.

$$

1 Trim photos to 2 by $2^3/4$ inches. Cut two $3^1/2$- by $4^1/2$-inch pieces paperboard and one $1^1/2$- by $3^3/4$-inch piece paperboard. Cut two $5^1/2$- by $6^1/2$-inch pieces and one $3^1/2$- by $5^3/4$-inch piece decorative papers. Center paperboard on the wrong side of each decorative paper and glue. Fold over the corners and glue, then fold over the sides and glue. Crease folds well with tool or spoon. Glue smaller, wrapped piece to the front of one of the larger pieces to form the box lid.

2 Cut three 3- by $4^1/4$-inch pieces cardstock. Embellish as you like with a gold pen, photo corners, or rubber stamps.

3 Line up covered paperboards, wrong sides up, with a bit of space between. The final section will be the bottom of the accordian package and needs to be placed upside down. Cut piece ribbon long enough to go behind whole row (ours measured 12 inches). Glue one end of ribbon to the back of the bottom piece. Glue a cardstock piece on top. Repeat with the other pieces. Glue the remaining ribbon to the back of the package *front*. Glue each photo to cardstock.

4 Cut 3- by $4^1/4$-inch piece cardstock. Write a holiday greeting. Glue the greeting to the back of the package's last section. All photos and your greeting should be facing you at this point.

5 Cut 10-inch piece gold cording. Form loop and glue to the back of package. Decorate if you like with a small button or silk flower.

6 Accordion-fold photo cards up into the package. Wrap package with ribbon and tie with a bow.

Angel Tree Topper

Create this angel from items around your home and craft supplies stored in your closet. It looks adorable on top of your tree and costs very little.

Materials

- 2-inch Styrofoam ball
- Clear half-liter bottle
- 4 yards each yellow and white cotton yarn
- Foam finish
- Craft stick
- Small cardboard box
- Acrylic craft paint: flesh, mauve, black
- 1 yard tulle netting
- White thread
- Gold chenille stem
- Tiny white satin bow
- Tiny white silk rose
- 3- by 10-inch white interfacing

Tools

- Double-end stylus
- Disposable bowl
- 1-inch foam brush
- Flat craft brush
- Liner brush
- Cotton swab
- Pair metal knitting needles
- Four clothespins
- Oven
- Straightedge
- Scissors
- Wire cutters
- Craft knife
- Sewing needle
- Hot glue gun and glue stick
- Pencil
- Oval template, 2 by 2½ inches

1 To create head, press ball onto bottle top (lid off), leaving a dent. Place ball on stylus. Pour foam finish into bowl and mix with craft stick until smooth. Using foam brush, apply finish evenly to ball. Stick stylus into cardboard box to allow finish to drip while drying. When head is dry, paint with flesh color. Using stylus and black paint, make dots for eyes. Make dots for mouth and pull into an oval. Using liner brush, add black eyebrows. Dip cotton swab into mauve paint and lightly touch on cheeks.

2 To make the hair, tightly wrap cotton yarn around metal knitting needles and secure ends with clothespins. Bake at 200 degrees for 30 minutes. Allow to cool. Remove yarn from knitting needles. Cut into 3-inch pieces. Make bundle and tie in the center with one piece of yarn. Glue yarn bundle on top of head and fluff. Using wire cutters, cut 6-inch piece chenille stem. Leaving 1¼ inches straight, form rest into circle. Press halo into top of head.

3 To make the body and dress, using craft knife, cut bottle 6½ inches from top. Cut two 6- by 36-inch pieces tulle. Using needle and thread, gather along long edge of one piece, ½ inch from edge. Glue around neck of bottle. Gather other piece 1 inch

from top. Glue over the other piece. Glue head to top of bottle. Glue bow and rose at the chin.

4 To make the wings, using pencil and template, trace two 2- by 2½-inch ovals side by side on the interfacing. Pinch centers together and secure with 2-inch piece of chenille stem, trimming the ends. Glue wings to back of angel's neck.

Wish Garland

Inspire your friends and family with a decorative garland expressing your hopes, dreams and wishes for them at the holiday season. Use the ribbon to decorate a wreath or Christmas tree.

$

Materials

- 9 feet (3/8-inch) light-colored holiday ribbon
- Craft beads
- Assorted glass beads
- 9 feet (20-gauge) gold wire
- Scrap paper
- Gel pen (dark color)

Tools

- Yarn darner (14/18)
- Wire cutters
- Pencil

1 Thread ribbon into the yarn darner. Pull through 2 inches. Using the darner, pull craft beads onto the ribbon, spacing every 8 inches. Knot the ends of the ribbon.

2 Cut 6-inch pieces of gold wire. Select groups of glass beads, varying sizes, colors, and shapes. Thread beads onto wire; twist wire tightly around ribbon to decorate.

3 On paper, write ideas for wishes. Pick your favorites and practice writing them in a flowing script. Using the gel pen, and anchoring the ribbon with two fingers, write the wishes on the ribbon.

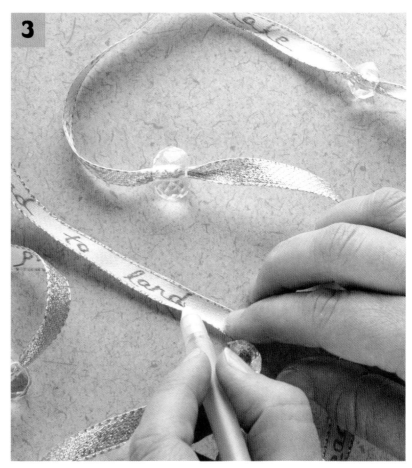

Stocking Ornament

Embroider a simple tree design on a cotton batting stocking for a natural look. The rickrack adds punch.

Materials

- 10- by 20-inch natural cotton batting
- Transfer paper
- Fabric marker
- Embroidery floss in green, red, and gold
- Embroidery needle
- ½ yard (½-inch) red rickrack
- Off-white thread
- Liquid seam sealer

Tools

- Copy machine
- Dressmaker's transfer wheel
- Scissors
- 8-inch embroidery hoop
- Pins
- Sewing machine
- Sewing needle

1 Enlarge stocking pattern 125%. Cut two 10- by 10-inch pieces batting. Trace stocking pattern with dressmaker's transfer paper and wheel, onto one piece but do not cut out.

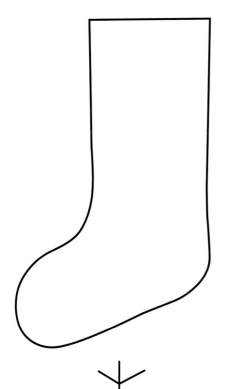

Transfer the tree design to the stocking the same way.

2 Put fabric in hoop. Using 2 strands of green floss, backstich the trunk, branches, and leaves. Using red floss, make a French knot at the end of each branch. Using gold floss, sew a star on top.

3 Place stocking front on top of the other piece of batting, pin, and cut out both pieces together. Place rickrack along top of each piece, a bit hanging over the sides. Pin so the bumps stick over the edge. Machine stitch close to the edge. Trim ends and apply seam sealant.

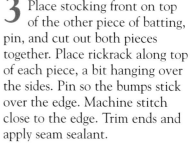

4 Place stocking pieces right sides together. Pin, pinning often around curves. Stitch, starting and ending 1½ inches from top edge. Turn cuff down. Cut 4-inch piece rickrack and form hanging loop; hand stitch inside cuff.

Woven Ribbon Pillow

With all of the beautiful ribbons available today, each ornament you weave can be a one of a kind. To further personalize a pillow, try sewing a letter or other meaningful charm in the center.

$

Materials

- Square white felt
- Narrow ribbons, variety of colors and types
- White thread
- Small beads or jingle bells
- Fiberfill stuffing
- Braid
- Tassel (optional)
- Beads (optional)

Tools

- Straightedge
- Scissors
- Pins
- Sewing machine
- Sewing needle
- Hot glue gun and glue stick

1 Cut two 6-inch squares felt. Cut a total of 14 (6-inch) pieces of assorted ribbons. Cross two ribbons in center of one piece of felt and pin.

2 Add more ribbons, weaving together and pinning as you go.

3 Hand-sew beads or jingle bells in the center and evenly along the edges.

4 Place woven piece on top of plain square. Cut 10-inch piece of ribbon for a hanger; make a loop and pin to one corner of ornament with the tails inside. Sew pieces together with a 1-inch seam allowance, leaving a small opening. Remove pins. Stuff pillow and hand-stitch closed. Trim pillow edges 1/4 inch from the stitching. Hot-glue braid around the ornament edge, covering the stitches.

5 If desired, add a tassel. Bring a needle and thread through the center of the tassel loop. String on some beads if you like. Stitch tassel to corner opposite the hanging loop.

Chapter 2

Deck the Halls

Christmas
Countdown
Calendar

Warm Hands Advent Calendar

Fill the mittens on this Advent calendar with candies or "good deed" suggestions. The mittens can be removed, so you can either add a mitten each day or leave all mittens hanging and remove the treats each day.

$$

Materials

- ¼ yard (72-inch) felt, white or light color
- 20 feet (¼-inch) ribbons, variety of colors
- Thread to match ribbons
- 25 (½-inch to ⅝-inch sew-through) buttons in assorted primary colors
- ⅜ yard double-sided fleece or felt
- ¼- or ⅜-inch dowel
- 25 (1¼-inch) tags, assorted colors as desired

Tools

- Copy machine
- Scissors
- Fabric marker
- Pins
- Fabric glue
- Books or other weights
- Straightedge
- Sewing needle
- Sewing machine (optional)
- Liquid seam sealer
- Permanent marking pen

1 Enlarge mitten pattern 125%. Trace a row of 25 mittens across the felt, making dots rather than lines. Cut whole strip and place on top of the rest of felt. Pin center of each mitten.

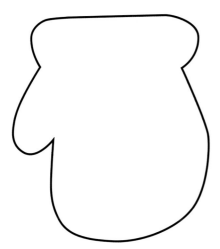

Cut mittens in pairs so both pieces will be the same.

2 Glue mittens together around all edges except the cuff. Press with the weight of books and allow to dry.

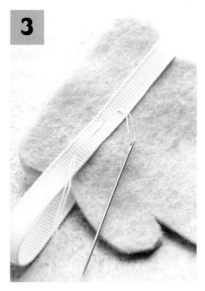

3 Cut 25 8-inch pieces ribbon. Apply liquid seam sealer to ends and allow to dry. For each mitten, pin a ribbon around the cuff indentation, starting in back and forming a 1-inch loop at the top of cuff. Attach ribbon with fabric glue or hand stitch using matching thread, making sure to keep cuff open. (**Tip:** Keep needle threaded with each color.)

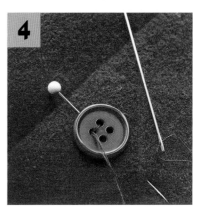

4 Cut 12- by 48-inch piece fleece or felt. Make a casing by folding shorter edge 1½ inches and stitching by machine or hand. Arrange mittens in eight rows of three plus one. Mark placement of buttons. Sew on by hand with matching thread, putting a straight pin behind the button so it will be loose enough for the ribbon loop.

5 Using permanent marker, number tags 1 through 25 and attach to buttons.

6 Insert dowel into casing. Cut 24-inch piece ribbon and tie at each end of dowel to create a hanger. Finish ribbon ends with liquid seam sealer. Hang mittens on the buttons.

Felted Stockings

Can't knit but love felted wool? Start with an old sweater from your closet or a thrift store. Either side of the felted fabric can go on the outside. Sometimes the wrong side is fuzzier and more textured. Embellish the stocking with beads or buttons, or even sew on a pocket made of a piece of the sweater.

Materials

- Large, 100% wool, pullover sweater
- Matching thread
- Old pillowcase or mesh laundry bag
- Matching yarn
- Beads, trims (optional)

Tools

- Copy machine
- Scissors
- Sewing machine
- Washer and laundry soap
- Baking soda (optional)
- Old bath towel
- Large-eyed sewing needle

1 Enlarge stocking pattern 400%. Place pattern on sweater, 3 or 4 inches from the bottom of the sweater. Pin around outside edge through both layers of sweater.

2 Using matching thread, sew around side and bottom with a medium zigzag stitch. Trim to ½ inch.

3 Place stocking pieces in old pillowcase and close with rubber band, or use mesh laundry bag. Wash on regular cycle, hot wash and cold rinse, with a small amount of laundry soap. Add a couple of old items such as T-shirts to balance the load. If the water is hard, add some baking soda to wash and rinse cycles. Place stocking on towel and block. Pull or pound out any wrinkles. Allow to dry.

4 Using matching yarn, sew a couple of large loops on the inside of stocking on heel side for hanging. Embellish stocking with beads or trims if you like.

5 You can also make a stocking with a contrasting cuff made from another sweater, a collar, or a ribbed edge. Cut out the stocking pieces without adding extra inches to the top. After felting and sewing, measure the top edge of the stocking. Cut a piece that long and 3 to 4 inches wide. Sew short ends of cuff together. Place cuff into stocking, right side to wrong side and pin. Machine or hand stitch. Turn cuff to right side.

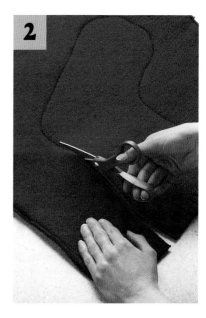

Family Photo Garland

Precious faces and family memories are the main ingredients for this personalized papercraft. Create small close-ups of faces with a digital camera and computer, or use a copy machine to enlarge photos and then crop them.

$$

Materials

- Family photos
- Three sheets decorative paper
- Black card stock
- Thick red cording
- Artificial berries and leaves

Tools

- Computer and printer or copy machine
- Straightedge
- Pencil
- Scissors, decorative-edge
- Glue stick
- Stapler
- Wire cutters
- Hot glue gun and glue stick

1 Using decorative scissors, trim photos to 2 by 2 inches. Using the glue stick, attach the photos to card stock. Trim stock to create a ¹/₂-inch frame.

2 For each photo, with decorative scissors cut rectangles from three papers: 2⁵/₈ by 4¹/₄ inches, 3¹/₈ by 4¹/₂ inches, and 3³/₈ by 4³/₄ inches. Stack. Glue.

3 Form a tube at the top of each paper stack by folding over 1³/₈ inches. Staple. Hot-glue photos in centers.

4 Using wire cutters, cut berries into pieces. Glue berries and leaves to the tops.

5 Slide the frames onto cording, positioning them 2 inches apart. Dab hot glue inside the paper tube to attach the frame. Cut cording leaving 7 extra inches on each end. Loop back the extra and glue to picture on the end to form hanging loop.

Square Mixed Greens Wreath

For a change, make a square wreath! To the pine base add greens in many shades, not necessarily traditional Christmas ones. Roses create the focal point; poinsettias could be used instead. Craft stores sell plain square wreaths; you could also square up a round wreath by forming corners against the corner of an old table.

$$

Materials

- Square pine wreath
- 1 yard wire-edged sheer ribbon
- Stems of artificial greens such as olive, juniper, sage, cedar, holly
- Rose stem with at least three blossoms plus buds
- Gypsophila

Tools

- Scissors
- Wire cutters
- Hot glue gun and glue sticks

1 To make a hanger, turn the wreath over and tie the ends of the ribbon to the top corners.

2 Bend and shape the pine to look natural (wear gloves to protect your hands). Using wire cutters, cut pieces from the greens. Arrange on the wreath, leaving the top side empty. Stick the pieces into the evergreen, wrapping with the pine, and hot-glue in place.

3 Cut roses into individual stems with leaves. Arrange a group at the center of the top. Insert into the pine and hot-glue.

4 Cut small pieces of gypsophila. Insert around the wreath.

Snowman Jester Stick

Jingle all the way! Prop this charming jester snowman against your doorway to welcome the holidays.

$$

46

Materials

- 1 yard (³/₄-inch) dowel
- Acrylic craft paint: white, red
- Clear finish spray
- 6-inch Styrofoam ball
- ²/₃ yard white polar fleece
- 12 inches string or ribbon
- ¹/₃ yard plaid polar fleece, at least 40 inches wide
- ¹/₃ yard double-sided polar

- fleece, red/blue
- Red thread
- 16 (¹/₂-inch) silver bells
- Five (⁷/₈-inch) gold bells
- Four large red bells
- Square orange felt
- Bit of polyester fiberfill
- Seven (¹/₂-inch) black pom-poms

Tools

- Brush
- Painter's tape
- Sewing needle
- Hot glue gun and glue stick
- Black permanent marker

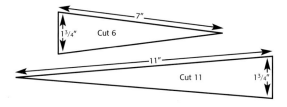

7"

1³/₄"   Cut 6

11"

Cut 11   1³/₄"

1 Paint dowel white, two coats. Allow to dry. Spiral tape along dowel. Paint exposed wood red, two coats if necessary. Allow to dry. Remove tape. Seal with clear finish spray.

2 Push dowel halfway through ball. Remove dowel. Squirt generous amount of hot glue into the hole, tilting so some drizzles down. Immediately insert dowel and twist. Cover ball with white fleece. Gather, pull down, and tie tightly with string or ribbon. Cut off all but 2¹/₂ inches fleece at the bottom.

3 To make the jester collar, cut 3- by 10-inch piece of two-

sided fleece and hot-glue around neck. Enlarge patterns 400%. Cut 11 large triangles and 5 small triangles of two-sided fleece. Sew five gold bells to the bottom of five large triangles. Red side facing out, hot-glue triangles around neck. Sew six silver bells to bottom of six large triangles. Hot-glue, blue sides out, between points of first layer. Sew six silver bells to bottom of six small

triangles. Hot-glue, red sides out, between points of second layer.

4 To make hat, cut 12- by 40-inch piece plaid fleece. Fold in half the long way, right sides together, and pin. With black permanent marker, mark long sides of fleece into tapered stocking-cap shape. Cut. Sew together. Fold up the bottom of the polar fleece 2 inches; pin and stitch. Turn hat right side out.

5 To make the scarf, cut 6- by 28-inch piece plaid fleece. Fold lengthwise, right sides together, and pin. Sew the long seam, leaving both ends open. Turn scarf right side out. Cut ends into fringe. Wind scarf around the snowman's neck and knot. Decorate the knot by sewing on three large red bells and hot-gluing four small silver bells.

6 Position cap on head, turning up band. Fold tip of cap forward and bunch. Sew a large red bell to the tip of the cap. Sew down tip of hat.

7 To make a carrot nose, cut 3- by 3-inch piece orange felt; fold in half and pin. Sew from the outside edge to the fold. Cut away excess fabric, and turn right side out. Fill with polyester fiberfill, then sew the nose closed. Sew to face. Hot-glue two pom-poms for the eyes and five pom-poms for the mouth.

Holiday Stripes and Bells Stocking

Wool felt is so easy to work with that it makes the ideal fabric for this quick holiday stocking. Be sure to use real wool felt, not craft felts.

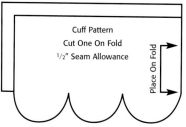

Cuff Pattern
Cut One On Fold
1/2" Seam Allowance

Place On Fold

Stocking Pattern
Cut Two
1/2" Seam Allowance

Materials

- Wool felt: 1/2 yard green, 1/4 yard each gold and red
- Green thread
- 3 (20-mm) jingle bells

Tools

- Copy machine
- Rotary cutter and mat
- Straightedge
- Fabric marker
- Sewing machine
- Sewing needle

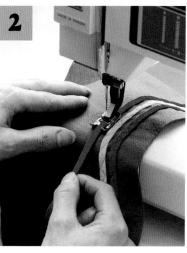

3 With right sides together, stitch stocking front and back together with a 1/2-inch seam allowance. Clip curves and turn right side out. With right sides together sew side seam on cuff.

will be the position of the first strip. Set machine for zigzag or serpentine stitch 4 mm wide and 2 mm long. Sew strips to stocking, threading them through the opening in the pressure foot and leaving a presser-foot width between each strip. Work from the right to the left to 1 inch from cut edge. Repeat on the other stocking piece.

1 Enlarge pattern 400%. Cut two stockings and one cuff from green felt. Using a rotary cutter, mat, and ruler, cut eight 1/4-inch strips each of gold and red felt.

2 With the straightedge, draw a line 1 inch from the right cut edge of each stocking piece. This

4 For a hanger, cut 3/4- by 6-inch strip of felt. Fold in half lengthwise and baste to wrong side of stocking top, with cut edges together. With right side of cuff facing wrong side of stocking, place cuff inside stocking, aligning side seam and top edges. Stitch a 1/2-inch seam. Turn cuff to outside.

5 Hand-sew jingle bells to cuff.

Christmas Countdown Calendar

Counting down the days until Christmas is fun at any age. Turning the page each day will provide a moment of reflection with inspiring quotes or perhaps a line from a favorite Christmas carol.

$$

Materials

- Flip-style photo stand
- 4 (8½- x 11-inch) sheets red, sage and dark green card stock
- 6 (8½- x 11-inch) sheets ivory cardstock
- Large holiday sticker
- Sheet decorative paper

Tools

- Straightedge
- Paper trimmer
- ¼-inch paper punch
- Tacky glue
- Scissors, regular and decorative-edge
- Computer and printer
- Double-stick foam tape
- 1⅞-inch x 1¼-inch oval paper punches

1 Remove screws from photo stand. Remove and measure front cover. Using paper trimmer, cut two pieces of card stock this size. Place cover over card stock and mark holes; punch. Glue card stock to both sides of front cover. Cut a different card stock ¼ inch smaller on all sides; glue to center front. On computer, type "Christmas Countdown Calendar" and print on a third card stock. Trim and glue to front cover. Press a sticker onto card stock and trim leaving a ¹⁄₁₆-inch border. Using double-stick foam tape, attach sticker to front of calendar.

2 Cut decorative paper size of back of the photo stand plus 1 inch of length. Glue paper to stand, wrapping over edges.

3 Cut 25 pieces card stock the size of a photo page. Mark and punch holes at the top of the pages. Type 25 Christmas messages and print on ivory card stock. Trim, then glue to coordinating card stock. Trim, leaving ¼-inch border. Decorate pages with pieces of leftover card stock, cutting them into strips or using punches. Glue message to center of each page.

4 Print large decorative numerals 1 through 25 on card stock, leaving space between. Cut with oval punch. Punch larger ovals from a coordinating card stock. Glue numbers on larger ovals. Glue numbers to bottom of each page. Put number 1 on the left edge of the first page, and each number further to the right until number 5 is at the right side. Repeat for other numbers. Put pages in order, put cover on top, and reassemble photo stand.

Festive Fruit
Card Holder

This decorative mailbox will hold all your holiday greetings in real style. Buy the mailbox in your hardware store. Choose a swag and candle ring to coordinate with the rest of your holiday décor.

$$$

Materials

- Green metal mailbox
- 20-inch fruit swag
- Large candle ring
- Gold bead garland

Tools

- Gold leafing pen

1 Wash the outside of the mailbox to remove any oils. Allow to dry. Using the gold leafing pen, write "Greetings" or another festive word or phrase on the side of the mailbox. Work from top to bottom to avoid smearing the lettering. If you like, outline the door, door opening, or flag. Allow to dry.

2 Put up the flag. Hook the end of the swag over the flag. Bend the swag over the mailbox toward the back end, arranging as desired.

3 Open the door of the mailbox flat. Place the candle ring on the inside of the door, bending if necessary to fit.

4 Drape the garland over the swag and candle ring. Fill mailbox with holiday greeting cards.

Winter Wonderland Birdhouse

Create a frosty, silvery birdhouse to glisten on a table. Buy an unpainted, decorative birdhouse at a craft store. You can surround the birdhouse with artificial snow and glittery holiday picks.

$$

Materials

- Decorative birdhouse
- White acrylic paint
- Pearlizing medium
- Silver finish
- Tube iridescent white dimensional paint
- Silver glitter
- Plastic icicle garland
- Ivory and pearl berries with leaves
- White bird

Tools

- Brush
- Paper towels
- White glue
- Spoon
- Paper
- Hot glue gun and glue sticks

1 Paint birdhouse white. Allow to dry. Paint with pearlizing medium. Allow to dry.

2 Paint the roof silver, and immediately wipe away some paint with a damp paper towel, leaving silver in the grooves and around edges. Allow to dry.

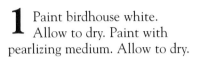

3 Paint edges of each side silver, immediately wiping with a damp towel to create a blended, shading look. Paint silver around the hole and perch, and wipe to soften the edges. Allow each side to dry before starting on the next side.

4 To put snow on the roof, squirt small amounts of dimensional paint along edges. Using your finger, smooth edges of paint up the roof. Allow to dry. If you like, build up a second coat.

5 Brush thin coat of glue on edges of the snow and sprinkle with glitter from a spoon, holding paper under the edge to catch the extra glitter.

6 Hot-glue berries and leaves to top of roof. Hot-glue bird to perch. Hot-glue some glittery leaves around the bird. Hot-glue

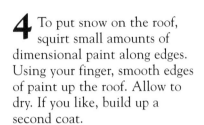

plastic icicle garland under the roof line and cut off any excess.

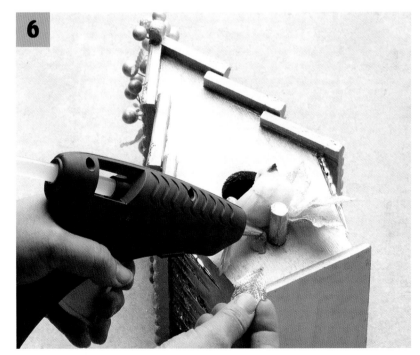

Holiday Door Bundle

This welcoming arrangement of holly, greens and frosted berries portrays a classic "Country Christmas" look.

Materials

- 14 inches gunnysack fabric
- Thread
- Block floral foam
- Coat hanger
- Holly bush
- Two stems frosted berries
- Two evergreen bushes
- Several large evergreen picks
- Plastic bags or packing pellets
- Rubber band
- 4 feet (2-inch) wired ribbon, holiday plaid or print

Tools

- Scissors
- Pins
- Sewing machine
- Serrated knife
- Wire cutters
- Floral tape
- Liquid seam sealer

1 Cut 13-inch by 26-inch piece fabric. Fold in half, right sides together, pin. Stitch side seams with two rows of zigzag stitches. Sew a line in zigzag 1 inch from the top of the sack. Pleat corners and stitch across pleating by machine or hand. This will give the bag a rounded, gathered corner. Fray 1 inch at the top by removing the horizontal threads. Turn bag right-side out.

2 Using the knife, cut ¾ of foam brick. With wire cutters, cut hanger at the outside

curves. Bend down the two remaining wires. At about 2 inches, bend them forward. Shape hanger's hook into an oval. Place brick on wire and attach with floral tape.

3 Insert holly bush in center of foam. Insert one berry stem in front off to the side. Insert an evergreen bush on each side. Insert berry stem in

the back. Fill in with evergreen picks.

4 Fill sack part way with crumpled plastic bags or packing pellets. Put floral arrangement into sack, gathering bag at base. Hold in place with rubber band. Tie ribbon around and make a bow. If ribbon may fray, put liquid seam sealer on the ends.

Northwoods Wreath

Decorate a small grapevine wreath with rustic shapes in a northwoods theme. Other nature-related shapes like birds will also work well. Look for birch bark on the ground when you are walking in the woods; do not remove it from live trees, as this harms them. Or purchase birch bark along with rusted tin shapes in craft stores.

$

1 Tear 1- by 22-inch strip fabric (snip selvage at 1-inch point and tear across the fabric). Tie in two places at top of wreath to form a hanger. Glue wreath on birch-bark square.

2 Arrange the tin shapes on the wreath, placing bits of torn bark behind some. Attach with hot glue.

Materials

- 6-inch grapevine wreath
- Scrap cotton fabric
- 6-inch square birch bark plus small strips
- Rusted tin shapes
- Fishing line

Tools

- Hot glue gun and glue stick
- Scrap wood
- Awl
- Hammer

3 Protect surface with scrap wood. Using awl and hammer, make a hole near the head of each fish. String fish on line. Tie line to wreath.

A Cup of
Christmas Cheer

Let your walls reflect the household's mood this Christmas. A brightly striped canvas makes the perfect base for this recipe of good cheer.

A Cup of Christmas Cheer

Start with heartfelt love. Combine equal amounts of holiday hugs and mistletoe kisses. Sprinkle liberally with laughter and garnish with warm wishes. Top off with friends and family. Serves everyone!

$$

Materials

- Canvas, 16 by 20 inches
- Acrylic craft paints: mint, dark green, bright pink
- White broad-tip paint pen
- Black fine-tip paint pen
- Four 1/2-inch wood buttons or tiny round balls
- Transfer paper
- 1/8 yard scrap canvas
- 5 yards cotton cording
- 2 1/2 yards (1/8-inch) green ribbon
- 1 yard (1 inch wide) grosgrain or satin ribbon

Tools

- Straightedge
- Pencil
- Masking tape
- Brushes: 3/4-inch, 1/4-inch, and fine
- Art eraser
- Fine sandpaper
- Copy machine
- Scissors
- Hot glue gun and glue sticks

1 Using straightedge and pencil, mark stripes of various widths across the 20-inch width of canvas. Place masking tape along the edge of the first line and paint; allow to dry. Paint rest of stripes with alternating colors, using tape to mask off painted and already dry stripes. Add white stripes with white paint marker.

2 Enlarge message 500%. Center message on canvas. Slide transfer paper under and secure with tape. Using a pencil, trace over letters. Paint letters with black paint pen. Erase any visible transfer lines. Lightly sand entire canvas.

3 Trace around holly pattern onto scrap canvas. Cut five leaves. Paint leaves mint green. Allow to dry. Paint veins and highlights dark green. Paint buttons pink. Allow to dry. Glue leaves and buttons to front of canvas as shown.

4 Cut cord in half, taping ends to prevent raveling. Twist ribbon and one piece of cording together, taping ends. Starting at bottom corner under the holly leaves, glue cording around edge of frame. Glue the second cord behind the first cord.

5 Fold ends of grosgrain ribbon under 1 inch and glue. Let dry. Glue ends of ribbon to back or side of canvas and let dry.

A Cup of Christmas Cheer

Start with heartfelt love. Combine equal amounts of holiday hugs and mistletoe kisses. Sprinkle liberally with laughter and garnish with warm wishes. Top off with friends and family. Serves everyone!

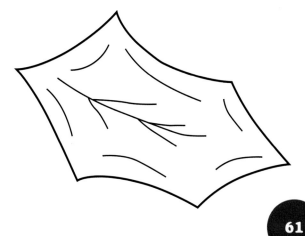

Peek-a-Boo Stockings

The clear pockets on this pair of stockings hold tiny treasures—stickers, beads, tiny toys... whatever your holiday heart desires.

$$$

Materials

- Felt squares: red, lime green, red polka dot, lime green polka dot
- Fabric marker
- 2-inch-square scrapbook sleeves
- Stickers and paper embellishments
- Tiny beads
- Glitter
- White thread
- 12 inches green cord
- Miniature ball ornaments, silver and red

Tools

- Copy machine
- Scissors
- Sewing machine
- Sewing needle

1 Enlarge stocking pattern 400%. Cut out. Trace pattern on dotted felt for each stocking front and back, and plain felt for four 6- by 3³/₄-inch cuff pieces.

2 Cut scrapbook sleeves apart, leaving small flaps. Holding pockets on point with the open ends up, fill with paper embellishments, beads, and glitter. Fold over flap and crease to secure.

3 Arrange pockets on stockings, down front or on cuff. Machine sew around the edges of each pocket.

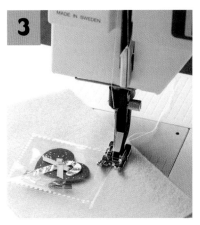

4 Pin cuff pieces to front and back of each stocking, extending ¹/₂ inch above top edge, wrong sides together. Zigzag stitch front and back together, leaving the top open. Add a second row of zigzag on the cuffs.

5 Make a loop with the cord; knot. Hand sew to top corner. Hand sew three ornaments near the knot.

63

Soft-Sculpture Snowman Pillow

"Build" an indoor snowman pillow that is soft and cuddly… and won't melt all over the floor!

Materials

- 1/3 yard (60 inches wide) each polar fleece: white, snowflake pattern, light blue
- 1/2 yard (60 inches wide) light blue polar fleece
- 9- by 12-inch square orange felt
- Thread: white, black, blue
- Polyester fiberfill
- Seven 1/2-inch black pom-poms

Tools

- Compass
- Permanent marker
- Scissors
- Pins
- Sewing machine
- Hand sewing needle
- Stick or skewer

1 To make head, fold white fleece in half, right sides together. Using the compass, draw a 6-inch-radius circle. Cut. Pin front and back of head together, right sides facing. Sew with 3/8-inch seam, leaving opening. Turn right side out. Fill generously with fiberfill. Sew opening closed.

2 To make hat, cut 12-inch square snowflake fleece. Fold in half, right sides together. Pin the two short sides together. Draw rounded edges on the corners next to the fold. Machine sew sides of hat and along curved markings with 3/8-inch seams. Trim curves. Fold edge of hat 1/2 inch and sew. Turn hat right side out.

3 To make nose, cut 4 1/2- by 4 1/2-inch square orange felt. Fold in half and pin. Draw line from the outside bottom edge to the middle of top. Sew along line, then trim. Turn nose right side out. Stuff, packing tightly with stick. Sew bottom of nose closed.

4 To make scarf, cut the blue fleece into 12- by 60-inch piece (use excess blue polar fleece to make the pom-pom.) Fold lengthwise, right sides together, and pin edges. Sew together with 3/8-inch seam, leaving ends open. Turn right side out. Cut fringe 2 1/2 inches long and 1/2 inch wide. Tie pairs

of fringe with double knots, pull so they twist into spirals.

5 To make hat pom-pom, cut fifteen 6- by 1/2-inch strips blue fleece. Cut one strip 10- by 1/2-inch and tie around the other strips in the middle.

6 Pin hat on head at angle. Turn up bottom edge, pin, hand sew. Hand sew around bottom of hat. Sew pom-pom on right corner of hat. Knot scarf around. With blue thread, sew scarf securely to snowman's head and along bottom of pillow. Using black thread, sew on black pom-poms for eyes and mouth. Using white thread, sew on nose.

Candy Covered Birdhouse

This makes a great family project—it involves fun and candy! Buy a decorative birdhouse at the craft store, cover it with frosting and candy, and display among greens or artificial snow. No special cake-decorating tools or skills are needed.

$$

Materials

- Wood or cardboard birdhouse
- 4 cups powdered sugar
- Three egg whites
- 1/8 teaspoon cream of tartar
- Assorted hard candies such as peppermints, gumdrops, holiday shapes

Tools

- Pencil
- Measuring cup
- Measuring spoons
- Large metal or glass bowl
- Electric mixer
- Paper towels
- Flexible-blade spatula
- Quart freezer bag
- Scissors

1 Unwrap the candy (good job for a child!). Decide where you want to place the candies. Using the pencil, mark the windows on the house.

2 Put sugar, egg whites, and cream of tartar in bowl. Beat on low for 5 to 7 minutes until icing is glossy and holds peaks. This icing dries quickly, so cover bowl with damp paper towels when not in use. (Let children know that this frosting is not for eating, as it contains raw egg whites.)

3 Prop the birdhouse with a dish or cutting board so the side on which you are working is fairly level. Using spatula, spread frosting smoothly over each surface. Start with each side of roof, then each side, then front. No need to do the back unless it will be part of a centerpiece. Immediately after icing a side, gently press candies into the frosting. Allow each side to set for 15 minutes in the level position before moving on.

4 Put frosting in bag and cut a bit off one corner. Squeeze bag to add a line of scallops to roof edges. Fill in any other areas needed, such as along corners of sides or roofline. Allow house to set overnight before handling.

Snowman Door Hanger

Create this adorable little snowman
using inexpensive materials or bits
from your scrap pile and button box.
Then hang from a doorknob or wall.
Finished height is about 13 inches.

$

Materials

- 14- by 16-inch natural cotton batting
- 14- by 7-inch piece muslin or other lightweight fabric
- 14- by 7-inch piece thick batting
- Buttons
- Matching thread
- Wire clothes hanger
- 14 inches wire
- Embroidery floss, matching or contrasting with batting
- Scraps of wool, felt, polar fleece, or other fabric
- Fabric glue

Tools

- Compass
- Paper
- Pencil
- Scissors
- Pins
- Sewing needle
- Wire cutters
- Masking tape
- Embroidery needle

1 Using compass, draw 7-inch, 6-inch, and 5-inch circles on paper. Cut out. Pin to cotton batting; trace; cut out for front of snowman. Arrange batting circles into snowman shape and pin together. Arrange paper circles the same way and tape; this becomes the pattern for the rest of the pieces. From cotton batting cut back of snowman slightly larger than pattern. From muslin cut one piece the size of the pattern. From thick batting cut one piece 1/4 inch smaller than pattern. Pull edges around natural-cotton circles for an uneven, fuzzy look. Sew buttons on face and down front.

2 Cut clothes hanger about 8 inches on each side of the center twist. Cut away top of hanger above twist. Place cotton batting back of snowman on surface and put muslin piece on top. Place wire at shoulder level to create arms. Bend arms as desired and twist end of wire into small loop that will later be covered with mittens. Tape arms to muslin. Put tape around top of hanger to protect muslin. Hand stitch arms in place. Create a hanging loop from the wire. Twist into loop leaving two long ends to run along the top of the head. Tape and stitch in place.

3 On top of snowman back/ muslin piece, stack thick batting and snowman front. With two strands of embroidery floss,

work a running stitch or backstitch around edges. This stitching does not need to be perfect; in fact, irregularities are part of the design and charm.

4 Cut hat, scarf, belt, and mittens from scrap fabrics. Using fabric glue, glue mittens together, then glue onto arms. Sew or glue rest of clothes onto snowman.

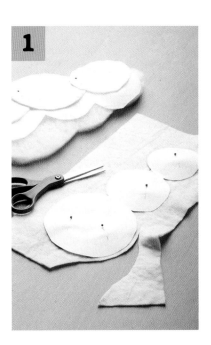

Chapter 3

Set Your Table

Mitten Silverware Holder

Create a fun and festive table with mitten silverware holders. The project makes one mitten; repeat as necessary. If you don't have a sewing machine, just use fabric glue.

$

Materials

- ½ yard royal blue washable felt
- Thread: blue, white
- ½ yard white fake fur
- Three snowflake buttons

Tools

- Copy machine
- Scissors
- Pins
- Sewing machine or fabric glue and clothespins
- Sewing needle

2 Cut two 2- by 4-inch pieces fur. Place at top of mitten for a cuff. Stitch or glue at sides only.

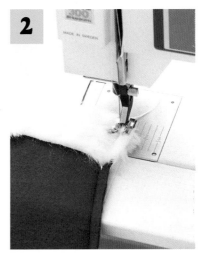

1 Enlarge mitten pattern to 150%. Cut out. Cut felt in half and place one piece on top of the other. Pin together. Place pattern on top and pin. Cut out mitten front and back together. Stitch pieces together with ¼-inch seam allowance, leaving top open; alternatively, apply glue around edges and secure with clothespins until dry.

3 Hand sew buttons on front. Insert silverware into mitten.

Snowman Placemat and Napkin Holder

Snowmen are always a hit, so create these placemats for any fun holiday gathering. The project makes one placemat, so repeat until you have enough. Choose washable wool felt.

$

Materials

- ½ yard royal-blue felt
- Felt squares: white, red, orange
- Thread: white, royal blue, orange
- Two ¾-inch red buttons
- Five ¼-inch white buttons

Tools

- Fabric marker
- Straightedge
- Scissors
- Pins
- Copy machine
- Sewing machine
- Sewing needle

1 Cut 12½- by 17-inch piece blue felt for one placemat. Cut 4- by 6-inch piece white felt. Cut 1- by 13½-inch piece red felt. Cut 1-inch square orange felt.

2 Place row of pins 1 inch from the short edges of the placemat. Cut ¼-inch fringe to the line of pins. Remove pins. Cut fringe ⅛ inch wide by ½ inch long across short ends of red felt.

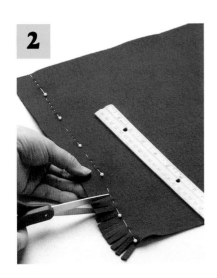

3 Enlarge snowman pattern 150%. Cut out and pin to white felt. Trace around pattern with marker. Cut out snowman. Pin snowman to lower left corner of placemat with red scarf behind neck area. Cut out nose pattern and pin to orange felt. Cut out carrot nose and pin to top of snowman. Carefully sew around snowman and nose.

4 Hand sew red buttons as earmuffs. Hand sew white buttons randomly on placemat as snow. Using scarf ends, tie a napkin onto placemat.

Snowmen Table Runner

Pop in your favorite holiday movie and have fun stitching up an heirloom that your family will enjoy for many years to come.

Materials

- ¹/₂ yard (36 inches wide) dark-blue felt
- 9- by 12-inch felt squares (one of each color): orange, yellow, red, hot pink, turquoise, lime green, black, purple
- 4 (9- by 12-inch) ivory felt squares
- Two skeins ivory embroidery floss

Tools

- Straightedge
- Embroidery needle
- Copy machine
- Fabric marker
- Pins
- Iron
- Scissors

1 Cut 3-foot by 18-inch piece blue felt. Fold corners until they meet in the center, and pin. With slightly warm iron, press the folds, and then cut off triangles. Fold over all edges of runner ¹/₂ inch and press.

2 Using two strands of embroidery floss, blanket stitch around edge. Insert needle from right side of fabric through hem to back. Bring needle up while holding the loop of thread with left thumb. Make a vertical stitch, bringing the needle out over the loop made by the thread. Pull needle through until the blanket stitch is snug against the fabric.

3 Enlarge patterns 400%. Cut out. Trace around patterns onto felt. Cut four snowmen and enough clothing for each one, mixing up the colors. Cut squares of contrasting colors to add to the scarves and mittens. Cut nine 1-inch round turquoise circles.

4 Place a snowman in each corner of runner, facing the middle. Pin. Using 2 strands of embroidery floss, sew on all pieces with blanket stitches, straight stitches, or big Xs. Place circles here and there and sew them to the runner with a 6-line "asterisk" snowflake design.

5 Cut four large white snowflakes from pattern. Cut four 4-inch turquoise squares. Using two strands of embroidery floss, sew large snowflakes to the squares, trim around the snowflake edges, then sew squares to runner as pictured.

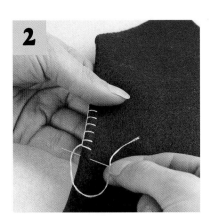

Earmuffs

Snowman

Scarf

Nose

Hat

Mitten

Snowflake

Mitten Chair Cover

Enjoy this adorable chair cover during the holidays … and all winter long!
Make matching Mitten Silverware Holders (page 72) for a total festive
look. If you don't have a sewing machine, secure the side seams with fabric
glue. These instructions are for one chair cover, so multiply as necessary.

$$

Materials

- 2 yards royal-blue washable felt
- Thread: blue, white
- 1/3 yard white fake fur
- Six snowflake buttons

Tools

- Tape measure
- Newspaper
- Pencil
- Scissors
- Pins
- Sewing machine or fabric glue and clothespins
- Sewing needle

2 Cut two 6- by 25-inch pieces fur. Place on mitten as a cuff. Stitch or glue at sides only.

3 Hand sew buttons on front. Place cover over chair.

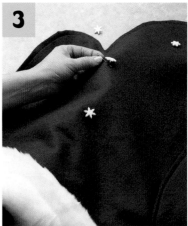

1 Measure height and width of chair back. Add 4 inches to width. Draw mitten shape on newspaper, including a thumb. Cut out pattern. Fold blue felt in half. Place pattern on felt and pin. Cut out mitten front and back together. Stitch pieces together with 1/4-inch seam allowance, leaving the top open; alternatively, apply glue around edges and secure with clothespins until dry.

Holiday Tea Light

Place this intriguing shade over a small glass jar holding a candle, then decorate your holiday table. Add a name tag to create a placeholder or favor. This tea light also makes a great gift.

$

Materials

- Sheet white card stock
- Sheet white vellum
- Circle template
- Square template
- Snowflake brass template
- Sheet snowflake paper
- 3¼ yards (⅛-inch) white satin ribbon
- Small candle in glass jar or baby-food jar and tea light

Tools

- Straightedge
- Pencil
- Craft knife
- Cutting mat
- Stylus
- Memory glue
- Scissors
- ⅛-inch punch

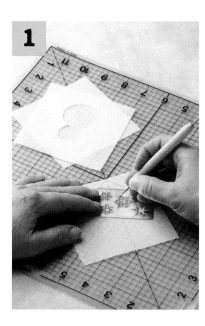

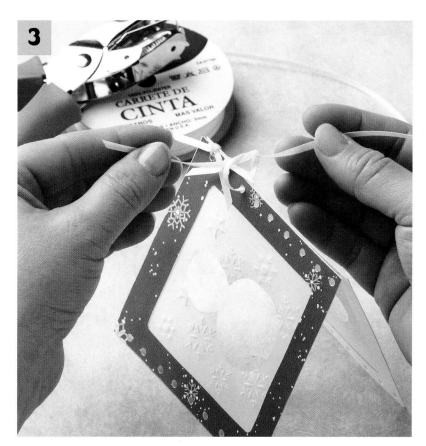

1 Using straightedge, pencil, craft knife and mat, cut four 4-inch square pieces card stock. Using square template, cut a 3-inch square from each center. Cut four 4-inch square pieces vellum. Using circle template, on each square of velum trace a 1-inch circle and 1½-inch circle in a snowman shape. Using craft knife, carefully cut out snowman shape. Using a stylus and brass template, randomly emboss snowflakes onto vellum.

2 Cut four 4-inch squares of printed paper. Using square template, center and cut a 3-inch square in the centers.

3 Glue card stock over vellum, and snowflake frames on top. Assemble the four sides to see which sides meet. Punch a row of holes on these sides only, approximately ¼ inch apart. Using scissors, cut ribbon into 4-inch pieces. Tie sides together and trim the ends. Set shade over candle jar.

Christmas Snowman Favor

Children can help make these fun favors, which can hold rock candy, jellybeans or any other small treat. The materials listed make one snowman; it's easy to make as many as you need.

$

Materials

- Small baby-food jar
- 2-inch Styrofoam ball
- Two black (1/2-inch) round buttons
- Square red glitter felt
- Bit of orange polymer clay
- Two blue (1-inch) pom-poms
- Two black 3/8-inch beads
- Fine-tip permanent marker
- 4 inches (20-gauge) gold wire
- Sheet white card stock
- 1/2 to 1 cup candy

Tools

- Glass glue
- Scissors
- Foam glue
- Craft knife
- Snowflake punch

1 Wash baby-food jar and remove label. Discard lid. Press ball onto jar opening. Take off and set aside. Using glass glue, attach buttons to front of jar.

2 Form clay into a carrot nose 3/4 inch long. Bake according to package directions.

3 Cut 3/4- by 12-inch strip felt. Fringe the ends, 1/8 inch wide and 3/4 inch long. Tie scarf around neck of jar.

4 Using foam glue, attach the nose, beads for eyes, and pom-poms for earmuffs. Draw eyebrows with the marker. Bend wire and insert between pom-poms to form the band of the earmuffs.

5 Cut 1 1/2- by 3-inch piece card stock. Punch a snowflake on one end. Glue cutout onto the scarf. Write name on card. Using craft knife, cut a slit in top of head. Insert card into slit.

6 Fill jar with candy. Set head on top.

Pieced Star
Table Runner

Create this table runner with fast cutting and piecing techniques. Select fabrics in holiday prints. The finished runner will be about 16 by 42 inches; you can add more blocks to make it longer.

$

Materials

- ¹/₈ yard (44 inches wide) cotton quilting fabric in print: red, dark red, light green
- ¹/₄ yard (44 inches wide) cotton quilting fabric in print: gold, dark green
- ⁷/₈ yard (44 inches wide) cotton quilting fabric in solid dark red
- ¹/₂ yard natural cotton batting
- Matching thread
- Gold embroidery floss

Tools

- Rotary cutter and mat
- Clear straightedge
- Yardstick
- Scissors
- Pins
- Iron
- Sewing machine
- Sewing needle
- Embroidery needle

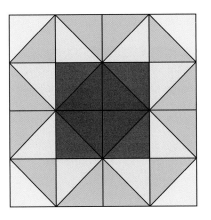

1 Prewash all fabrics. Cut 6 squares each of red, dark red and light green, 12 squares of gold and 18 squares of dark green. Each of the squares will be cut diagonally to create the triangles. Cut in the following manner: Stack dark green and gold together folded in half, as it comes on the bolt. Even up cut edge with long ruler and rotary cutter. Cut 2 (4-inch) strips, then cut into 4-inch squares to equal 12 gold and 18 dark green. Cut each square with a true diagonal. Hold

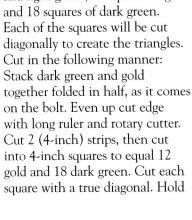

the ruler firmly for each cut. Stack the remaining fabrics, cutting one 4-inch strip and 6 squares each.

2 Arrange right sides together and stack the following pairs: 12 dark green and light green triangles; 12 dark red and red; 24 dark green and gold. Sew together with ¹/₄-inch seam as follows: Sew first pair together, then put next pair under foot and keep going. Clip pairs/blocks apart. Press seams toward light fabrics.

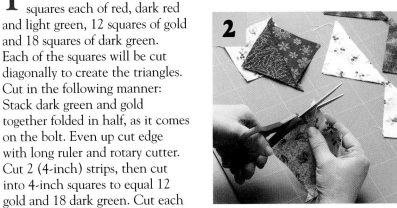

3 Arrange each block as shown. Stitch rows together. Press seam allowances to one side. Stitch rows together and press.

4 Square up blocks using clear straightedge and rotary cutter. Cut four 2¹/₂-inch strips of plain fabric. Cut four sashing pieces the height of a block. Pin and stitch sashing to one side of

each block and the final one to the end block. Press. Measure length of table runner at top, bottom, and in middle. Average this measurement. Cut remaining 2 strips that measurement. Pin and stitch to top and bottom of table runner and press. Measure table runner and cut batting and lining to the measurement.

5 Stack pieces from bottom: batting; pieced top, right side up; lining right side down. Pin. Stitch together, stopping 3 inches from one end. Clip seam allowance away from corners and turn. Push corners out, press. Turn under seam allowances in open area, press and slipstich closed. Press. Pin through table runner randomly to hold layers together. Tie square knots, using 3 strands of embroidery floss, at the center of block and star points.

Festive Votive Candles

Light each guest's place setting with embellished votive candleholders using scrapbooking supplies for a crisp and contemporary look. Remember: never leave candles unattended.

Materials

- Clear small glass votive candleholder
- One sheet patterned velum
- Three fancy dimensional stickers
- Votive candle

Tools

- Tape measure
- Straightedge
- Pencil
- Scissors
- Clear tape
- Hot glue gun and glue stick

3 Hot-glue stickers to cover the front paper seam and to decorate the candleholder. Add a votive candle.

1 Remove label from bottom of candleholder. Measure around candleholder and add ⅛ inch. Measure the height of the candleholder. Using straightedge and pencil, draw rectangle this size on the velum. Cut.

2 Apply small amount of clear tape at top and bottom of the paper seam, extending over top of holder to hold paper in place.

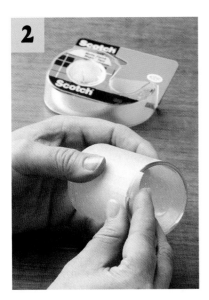

87

Country Winter Placemats

It's definitely a country Christmas when these placemats are on the kitchen table. The cutout shapes used as patterns are sold in craft and scrapbook stores.

$$$

Materials

- 2 yards tan imitation-suede fabric
- Matching thread
- Theme cutout shapes
- Felt squares: green, yellow, blue
- Assorted color brads
- Gold star-shaped brads

3

Tools

- Straightedge
- Scissors
- Pins
- Sewing machine
- Iron
- Sewing needle
- Fabric glue
- Paper piercer

1 For four placemats, cut eight 12- by 17-inch pieces fabric.

3 Pin cutout shapes on felt. Cut 3 green trees, 16 blue stars, and 3 yellow moons. Glue shapes to the placemats.

4 Using paper piercer, poke holes through the trees and the placemat behind. Insert brads as the ornaments. Insert a star brad on the top of each tree.

2

4

2 To make each placemat, place two pieces right sides together, edges even. Pin. Sew around edges with a ¼-inch seam, leaving 4 inches open. Turn right side out. Press seams under at opening. Slipstitch opening closed.

Gift Box
Napkin Holder

This little napkin holder becomes the centerpiece of each plate at your holiday table. Create as many as you need! You can also insert a little surprise through the hole for each person to discover when the napkin is removed. Find the box in craft stores.

Materials

- Cylinder-shaped paper-mâché box, 3¹/₂ inches high and 2³/₄ inches wide
- ¹/₈ yard each silver and green lamé fabric
- 1 yard (1¹/₄-inch) red wire-edged ribbon
- Two holiday evergreen picks

Tools

- Fabric glue
- Cotton swab
- Straightedge
- Fabric scissors
- Manicure scissors
- Compass
- Serrated knife
- Wire cutters
- Hot glue gun and glue stick

1 Using your finger, smooth thin layer of fabric glue on the top and sides of the lid. Lay lid on silver fabric. Smooth out any wrinkles or bubbles. Allow to dry. Trim fabric to 1 inch above edge. Cut some slits in the extra fabric up to the cardboard. Smooth glue inside the lid and fold over the fabric.

2 To make the napkin holes, draw a 1-inch circle in the center of opposite sides of the box. Cut out with a serrated knife. Smooth fabric glue on the box. Lay box on green fabric, with an overlapping seam in the back. Allow to dry. Wrap fabric over edges and glue. Fold fabric to bottom of box and glue.

3 Using manicure or fabric scissors, make eight cuts in the fabric covering the holes (as if you were cutting a pizza). Reach inside the box and spread glue around the hole. Fold over fabric and attach.

4 Put lid on box. With tape measure, measure around the box from top to bottom, and back up the other side. Cut piece of ribbon this size. Attach ribbon around box with hot glue. Cut 8-inch and 6-inch pieces ribbon.

Make two loops and glue, then glue smaller loop on the bigger one, and glue the set to the lid.

5 Using wire cutters, cut the long stem from holiday pick. Hot-glue the pick to lid. Fill in with bits of greenery or berries from the other pick. Pull a dinner napkin through the holes and set the holder on the dinner plate.

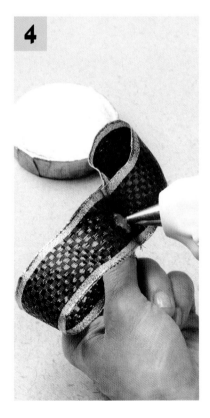

Christmas Reflections Table Setting

Stained glass and shining mirrors will give your table a very special holiday glow. Choose a 14-inch mirror for a centerpiece or 12-inch mirror for a charger plate.

$$

Materials

- Round mirror
- Clear glass
- Black liquid leading
- Glass paint: gold glitter, kelly green, green, red and white
- ¹⁄₂ yard red felt

Tools

- Copy machine
- Glass cleaner
- Tape
- Fine brush
- Pin
- Pencil
- Scissors, decorative-edge
- White tacky glue

3 Center mirror over felt and trace around with pencil. Cut felt with decorative scissors.

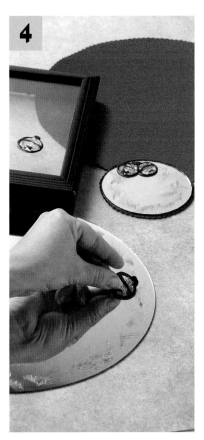

1 Enlarge patterns 250%. Cut out. Place patterns under glass and tape. Using liquid leading, trace patterns as many times as needed, moving patterns to new spots. Allow to dry. Fill in shapes with glass paint. Use pin to pop any bubbles in paint. Allow to dry.

2 Clean mirror with glass cleaner. Following diagram, paint pine boughs around the edge of the mirror. Start with darker green and allow to dry. Add kelly green. Allow to dry.

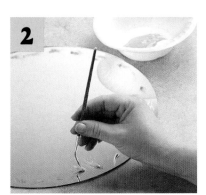

4 Liberally apply glue to back of mirror and press onto felt. Allow to dry. Carefully peel bows and bells from glass and press onto mirror, placing as shown.

So-Striped Table Mat

Create a soft spot for a bowl of Christmas candy or most any holiday accent. This ribbed felt mat uses all your favorite holiday hues, plus a few unexpected colors. Buy the square dowels at a craft or hardware store.

$$

Materials

- 8 (1-yard lengths) of ³/₈-inch square doweling
- Felt squares: green, red, lime green, white, black, purple, bright pink, turquoise
- ¹/₃ yard bright green felt
- Small bag ¹/₂-inch red pom-poms
- Small bag assorted 1-inch pom-poms: green, bright pink, turquoise, purple

Tools

- Saw
- Straightedge
- Pencil
- Scissors
- Hot glue gun and glue sticks

1 Using a saw, cut 23 1-foot pieces of dowel. Cover 21 of the dowels with felt. Cut 21 pieces, 1¼ by 12 inches, from a variety of felts. Wrap one around each dowel, gluing only at the long edges so glue will not show through.

2 Cut some 1³/₄- by 12-inch strips felt. Fringe the long sides of the strip.

3 Glue a felt-covered square dowel in the center of each fringed strip.

4 Cut 12- by 18-inch piece bright green felt. Position one of the two remaining dowels on on the short end of the felt. Roll dowel twice toward the center of the mat and glue in place. Glue felt-covered dowels side by side on top of the green felt, with all fringes pointing up. Roll and glue remaining dowel at far end.

5 Glue a red pom-pom on the end of every other dowel, skipping the first dowel. Fill in with larger pom-poms.

95

Christmas Gardener Centerpiece

Spruce up your holiday table by showing your passion for gardening and crafting in a playful and fresh way.

$$$

Materials

- Tin or metal watering can
- Spray paint: white, red
- 1/4-inch dowel
- Hand trowel, hand cultivator, handheld weeder
- Acrylic craft paints: white, yellow, green, blue, red, black, purple, brown, light gray
- Holiday greens

Tools

- Cotton swabs
- Craft paintbrushes
- Fine-tip permanent marker
- Spray finish, clear matte
- Hot glue gun and glue stick

1 Thoroughly clean the watering can and gardening tools if they have been used. Allow to dry. Spray tools white. Spray watering can red, two coats, allowing each coat to dry. Using a cotton swab, dab white paint on can to make dots. Allow dots to dry. Spray with matte finish.

2 Paint hand trowel handle orange with black polka dots. Paint hand trowel blade medium blue. Paint a snowman standing in snow. Dot snowflakes on sky with end of brush handle. Paint earmuffs, vest, stick arms, and scarf. Using light gray paint, outline snowman and make a shadow. Using fine marker, outline snowman and all details.

3 Paint handle of hand cultivator green. Paint neck red-and-white striped. Paint tines yellow. Paint thick white stripes on handle.

4 Paint handheld weeder blue. Paint neck red-and-white striped. Paint end of handheld weeder purple. Paint six-sided snowflakes on handle and add dots. Spray finish on both sides of the tools and the watering can. Allow to dry.

5 Measure height of can and add 2 inches. Cut three

dowels this size. Paint top inches of dowel same color as a gardening tool. Hot-glue top of dowels to bottom of tool handles.

6 Place holiday greens in can and arrange tools.

Wrapped Package Candleholder

This festive candleholder looks like a shiny gift-wrapped package. Make matching placecard holders, too!

$

Materials

- Scrap lumber
- White primer paint (optional)
- Silver paint
- $^7/_8$-inch candle cup
- $^1/_4$ yard lamé fabric or printed foil
- 2 yards ($^5/_8$-inch) wire-edged ribbon
- $^1/_2$ yard ($^3/_8$-inch) ribbon
- Thumbtacks, small heads

Tools

- Table saw or handsaw and miter box
- Sandpaper
- Brush
- Scissors
- Straightedge
- Transparent tape
- Wood glue
- Utility knife

1 Cut 3$^1/_2$-inch cube wood. (Note that a standard 4x4 is actually 3$^1/_2$ by 3$^1/_2$ inches.) Sand edges and corners. If fabric is partially see-through, paint wood with white primer. Allow to dry. Paint candle cups silver. Allow to dry.

2 Cut 8$^1/_2$- by 14-inch piece fabric or foil. Cut 1-inch hole in the center. Center wood cube on fabric. Fold as if wrapping package, securing with tape.

3 Using wood glue, glue candle cup to top center of package.

Allow to dry. Wrap ribbon around box up sides of box. Crease at the candle cup and cut ribbon. Tape ribbon in place. Repeat for other two sides of box. Cut four 6-inch and four 5-inch pieces ribbon. Form loops and secure with tape. Using thumbtacks, attach next to candle cup.

4 To make a placecard holder, cut 1$^3/_4$- by 3$^1/_2$-inch block wood. Cut $^1/_2$-inch-deep slit at a slight angle in top of block. Sand edges and corners. Paint wood with a white primer, if needed. Cut 8$^1/_2$-by 6-inch piece fabric. Wrap block as above. Using utility knife, cut fabric at the slit. Cut ribbon to go around shorter side of package. Tape ribbon at bottom of block. Cut 6-inch piece ribbon; form bow and secure with thumbtack.

Chapter 4

Gifts to Give

Wool Throw
Pillow Cover

Recycle old wool throws or stadium blankets into decorative pillows. The fringe is a great design detail.

$$

Materials

- Wool throw
- 18- by 24-inch square pillow form
- Thread
- Large button
- Yarn

Tools

- Tape measure
- Scissors
- Sewing machine
- Yarn needle

together, and the flap extends at the top. Stitch sides with 1/2-inch seam. Turn pillow cover right side out. Fold back and stitch 1/2-inch hem on edges of flap.

3 Insert pillow form and turn down flap. Close flap by hand-sewing button with yarn and yarn needle. Leave tails of yarn and tie yarn to secure button.

1 If necessary, wash throw in cold water, gentle cycle, and hang to dry. Determine which part of the throw you will use for the pillow. Center any dominant stripe or pattern.

2 Using tape measure, measure the width of the pillow form and add 1 inch. From the entire length of the throw, including fringe, cut a strip that wide. To determine cut length, place pillow form on one end of the strip. Pull over the top of pillow form as much material as you want for a flap (position so the fringe will be on the edge of the flap). Wrap the other end of the strip around the pillow. Mark cutting line with pins. Remove pillow form. Cut throw. Fold throw so pillow front and back come together, right sides

Decorative Coasters

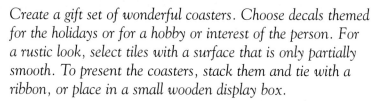

Create a gift set of wonderful coasters. Choose decals themed for the holidays or for a hobby or interest of the person. For a rustic look, select tiles with a surface that is only partially smooth. To present the coasters, stack them and tie with a ribbon, or place in a small wooden display box.

$$

Materials

- Six 4-inch shower tiles with smooth or partially smooth surface
- Decals
- Clear acrylic spray
- Adhesive-backed foam or felt

Tools

- Cloth
- Applicator from decal package
- Scissors

1

2

2 When all the tiles have decals, in a well-ventilated area, spray with several coats of clear acrylic spray, allowing to dry between applications.

3 Cut foam or felt ¼ inch smaller than tiles. Remove backing and apply to back of tile.

3

1 Dust tiles with damp cloth. For each tile, cut one or more decals from sheet. Position as you like, on a smooth area of the tile surface. Remove backing and place decal on tile. Using provided applicator, rub design onto tile, then carefully remove top paper. The decal will appear to whiten when it has adhered to the tile. If a portion of the decal did not stick to the tile, cover the decal with the top paper and continue to rub.

Simply Soup

Red, green, and white beans are the colorful ingredients of this gift of soup or chili. Add a gift tag with a recipe, and tie in a wooden spoon if you like. The materials listed make one soup kit, but this is a project designed to make in multiples for neighbors and friends.

$

Materials

- 12-inch icing bag
- ½ cup dried kidney beans
- ½ cup split peas
- ½ cup dried navy beans
- Small rubber band
- Wired evergreen pick
- 1 yard red ribbon
- Card stock
- Decorative paper
- Narrow ribbon

Tools

- Wire cutters
- Computer and printer
- Scissors, decorative-edge
- Hole punch

1 Fill bag with the three beans. Twist top tightly and wrap with rubber band.

2 Twist wire of decorative holiday pick around top of bag. Using the wire cutters, trim the extra stem.

Christmas Three-Bean Chili (pictured)

INGREDIENTS TO ADD

1 tablespoon oil
Medium onion, chopped
1 pound ground beef
14.5-ounce can peeled, crushed tomatoes
14.5-ounce can diced tomatoes
1 teaspoon chili powder
Pepper to taste
Garlic powder to taste

TO PREPARE THE BEANS

Put beans in a medium saucepan, cover with water. Boil 5 minutes. Remove from heat and let stand 30 minutes; drain.

TO MAKE CHILI

Heat oil in frying pan. Brown onions and beef. Add rest of ingredients including beans. Cover and simmer on medium low for 20 minutes. Makes 6 servings.

Christmas Three-Bean Soup

INGREDIENTS TO ADD

6 cups water
2 cups cooked turkey, chicken, or ham
Three carrots, chopped
Medium onion, chopped
Celery rib, chopped
14.5-ounce can peeled, crushed tomatoes
½ teaspoon salt
½ teaspoon pepper

TO PREPARE THE BEANS

Put beans in bowl and completely cover with water; soak overnight. Drain.

TO MAKE SOUP

Put all ingredients in pot. Bring to a boil. Reduce heat and simmer until carrots are soft, about 30 minutes. Makes 6 servings.

3 Type your holiday greetings and choice of recipe on computer. Print on card stock. Using decorative scissors, trim. With decorative scissors, cut larger piece paper. Glue recipe card on decorative paper. Punch hole in card. Put narrow ribbon through hole in card, tie around top of bag. Tie wide ribbon around the bag and make a bow.

Ribbon Candy Shirred Pin

These funky wool felt pins look just like holiday ribbon candy. Use them on slippers, sweatshirts, decor… anywhere that needs a holiday boost.

$$

Materials

- ¹/₄ yard each wool felt in three contrasting colors
- Iron-on adhesive
- Matching embroidery floss
- Matching thread
- 1¹/₂-inch pin back

Tools

- Compass or circle template
- Rotary cutter and mat
- Straightedge
- Fabric marker
- Size 24 tapestry needle or shirring needle
- Sewing needle

1 Soften the felt by washing each color separately in cold water and drying on the line. Using compass or circle template, cut two 2¹/₂-inch circles wool felt and one circle adhesive. Fuse two felt circles together with the adhesive, following manufacturer's instructions.

2 Using rotary cutter, mat, and straightedge, cut ¹/₂-inch strips felt. For flower center, cut 20-inch piece. For petals, cut 27-inch pieces of two other colors. Starting ¹/₄ inch from end, mark dots every ³/₄ inch down the center of one petal piece and flower center.

3 Thread tapestry needle with two strands embroidery floss. Hold the two petal pieces together. Sew running stitch down center of strips, passing down through one dot and up through the next dot. Repeat with flower center. Pull strips into flexible pleats. The piece for flower center will measure about 2 inches when pulled up, and the petal pieces about 7 inches. Tie knot at end to hold pleats.

4 Form smaller piece into a circle. Using the sewing thread, hand sew the ends together. Lay center of flower on its side and hand sew to base. Repeat with outside petals. Hand sew pin back to base back.

109

Matchbook Dream Journal

Personalize fun matchbook journals for many themes. These instructions create a small journal for anyone to record goals or dreams throughout the year. To make the winter journal shown, use rub-on snowflakes and two designs of snowflake punches.

Materials

- Card stock: lavender, purple, white
- Metallic gold paper
- Four sheets white copy paper
- Gold star brad
- Scrap purple printed paper
- 12 inches purple fuzzy yarn
- Paper daisy embellishment
- Sticker letters

Tools

- Scissors
- Straightedge
- Pencil
- Paper-scoring tool
- Tear edger
- 1/8-inch punch
- Memory Glue
- Flower-hole punch (optional)

1 To make the journal, cut 5- by 10½-inch piece lavender card stock. On a 5-inch side, score and fold up ¾ inch. From this fold line, measure 5⅛ inches and score and fold up again. Punch hole at the center of the spine. Cut eight 5-inch squares copy paper. Punch hole in each to line up with the hole in spine. Insert brad through all holes. Cut ¼- by 5-inch strip purple card stock. Glue strip above the brad along the spine.

2 To make the cover, cut 4½- by 4-inch piece gold card stock. Cut 3¾- by 4½-inch piece purple card stock. Glue purple piece in the center of gold piece. Cut 3-inch square purple printed paper. Using tear edger, tear square into triangle. Put glue along the straight edges of the triangle only and adhere to purple card stock leaving ¼-inch border of purple. Cut ¼- by 5½-inch strip lavender card stock. Glue to purple card stock ⅝ inch from torn edge of triangle. Glue daisy to triangle.

3 To make the tag, cut 1½- by 3-inch piece white card stock. On one end, trim ½-inch triangle from each side. Using regular or flower punch, punch hole and insert yarn and tie. Cut 1¼- by 2¼-inch piece lavender cardstock. Glue white piece on lavender piece. Cut ⅛- by 2-inch strip purple card stock. Glue to card. Adhere word of choice to tag. Insert tag into triangle pocket.

Personalized BBQ Apron

Make this apron personal with a themed print fabric. If you like, print a related photograph onto a special fabric sheet sold at the craft or fabric store and sew it toward the top of the apron.

$$

Materials

- 1 yard (60 inches wide) denim
- Matching thread
- ³/₈ yard print quilt fabric
- Four (³/₄-inch) D-rings

Tools

- Shears
- Rotary cutter and mat (optional)
- Yardstick
- Fabric marker
- Pins
- Iron
- Sewing machine
- Size 16 needle

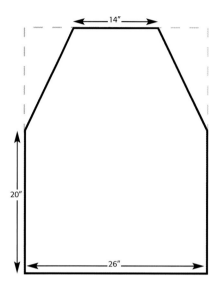

1 Cut 26- by 34-inch piece denim. Fold in half lengthwise. Along top, measure 6 inches from each side and mark. Along sides, measure 20 inches from bottom and mark. Connect the marks to create angled sides. Cut. Cut denim strips 2¹/₂ by 30 inches (neck tie), 2¹/₂ by 40 inches (waist tie), and 2¹/₂ by 6 inches (to hold D-rings). Cut 16- by 12-inch piece print fabric.

2 Press angled sides of apron ³/₈ inch, then again ³/₈ inch. Stitch along folded edge. At top of apron, press under ³/₈ inch, then 1 inch. Pin. Stitch along folded edge. For straight sides of apron, fold and press ³/₈ inch, then 1 inch. Pin but do not stitch yet. Do the same for bottom hem. Press up a triangle at the bottom corners. Trim to press line. Fold and pin corners, sides, and bottom. Stitch near folded edge.

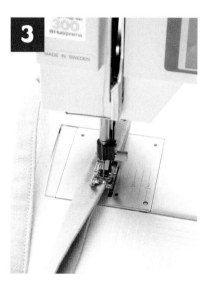

3 For each tie, fold one end ¹/₂ inch and press. Fold long edges ¹/₂ inch and press. Fold tie in half lengthwise and press. Pin. Stitch along edge. Stitch raw end of 30-inch tie at top right corner of apron on the back side. Repeat with longer tie at the waist. Cut shortest tie in half. Loop pieces around D-rings and stitch to the other sides of apron.

4 To make pocket, zigzag or serge all edges of print fabric. Fold bottom ¹/₂ inch and press. Fold sides ¹/₂ inch and press. Fold top 1 inch, press, and stitch ³/₄ inch from fold. Center pocket on apron 7 inches from bottom. Topstitch side and bottom near folded edges, reinforcing at the top with a "U" shape. (Contrasting thread used for visibility.)

113

Vintage Apron

This is a wonderfully
old-fashioned apron,
perfect for holiday
baking. Cotton quilting
fabric is a good choice.
The rickrack is not
only decorative, but
makes the edging easy.

$

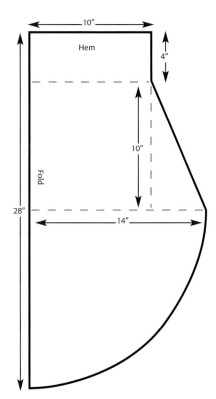

10"

Hem

4"

Fold

28"

10"

14"

Materials

- 1 yard (44 inches wide) lightweight cotton fabric in retro print, prewashed
- 3 yards ($1/2$ inch wide) coordinating rickrack
- Matching thread

Tools

- Newspaper or tissue paper
- Pencil
- Scissors
- Straightedge
- Pins
- Iron
- Sewing machine

1 Fold fabric in half lengthwise. Along top, measure 10 inches from fold and mark. Measure 4 inches down on sides, for hem, and mark. Along fold, measure 14 and 28 inches down; mark each point. Follow diagram to create angled and curved sides. For tie, cut two 3-inch by 30-inch pieces fabric along selvage edge. Mark pocket diagram on fold (see below); add $1/2$-inch seam allowance on side and bottom. Cut two pockets.

2 Serge or zigzag stitch all raw edges of fabric. On right side of fabric, align rickrack on apron edges, with 1 inch extending into top hem area. Pin. Stitch down

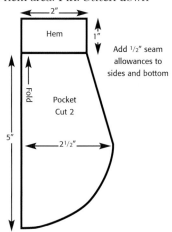

2"

Hem

1"

Add $1/2$" seam allowances to sides and bottom

Fold

Pocket
Cut 2

5"

$2^1/2$"

center of rickrack, stopping at hem area. Turn rickrack to wrong side of fabric; from right side, press. For main apron, topstitch on right side close to pressed edge. Repeat for pockets but do not topstitch. Turn short raw edges under $1/4$ inch and press; turn top edge down 1 inch and press. Angle the extended rickrack under the hem; pin and press. Starting $3/4$ inch from top folded edge, stitch pocket hems. Set pockets aside.

3 To make ties, turn and press a double $1/4$-inch hem on one long side. Stitch. Wrong sides facing, match raw end of tie with raw side edge, making diagonal fold; press doagonal fold. On raw long edge, press a double $1/4$-inch hem; stitch. Repeat with other tie.

4 Turn top of apron (waistband) down $3/8$ inch and press. Turn hem (waistband) to wrong side to meet top edges of the rickrack. Angle the rickrack under the hem. Press. Pin

unfinished end of tie here, taking a small tuck or pleat in the center of tie if necessary. Repeat on other side. From wrong side, stitch across tie, along the long folded edge, and across the other tie.

5 Place inside top corner of each pocket 3 inches from center of apron and 3 inches from stitching at waist hem. Pin. Topstitch pockets in place, stitching forward and backward at least $1/2$ inch at beginning and end for strength.

Beautiful Blooming Bookmarks

Tuck a bookmark into a novel as an extra, touch-of-class addition to the gift … or include a bookmark with each of your holiday greeting cards. Either way, these charming bookmarks will get rave reviews.

$

Materials

- 1/3 yard (5/8-inch) pale yellow grosgrain ribbon
- 1/3 yard (1-inch) turquoise or olive ribbon
- White thread
- 5/8-inch buttons: red, pink
- Mini buttons: purple, red, yellow, orange
- Olive green embroidery floss

Tools

- Straightedge
- Scissors
- Pins
- Sewing machine
- Sewing needle
- Embroidery needle

1 To make one bookmark, cut 7½-inch piece yellow ribbon and 9½-inch piece turquoise or olive ribbon. Center shorter ribbon on longer piece and pin. Using white thread and zigzag stitch, stitch along edges of yellow ribbon. Bring thread ends to back, knot, clip.

2 Turn ribbon ends twice. Hand sew with tiny stitches on back, catching the thread in the ribbon's ribs so stitches will not show on front.

3 Using photo for inspiration, sew buttons with white thread to look like a single bloom or group of flowers.

4 Using three strands green embroidery floss, sew lazy-daisy leaves around the button flowers. Stitch straight stems.

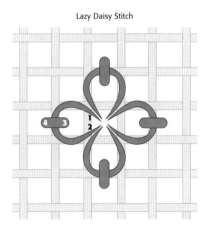

Lazy Daisy Stitch

Cell Phone Carrier

A tween on your list will love this funky carrier for her cell phone. The inside of the carrier will measure 3½ by 5 inches, which will fit most cell phones. Recycle the denim from the bottom of an old pair of jeans.

Materials

- Old pair jeans
- ¹/₃ yard ball fringe or other trim
- ³/₄ yard (¹/₂-inch) ribbon
- Matching thread for denim and trim
- Two clasps and circles
- Charms, decals, rhinestones, beads, or decorative pin

Tools

- Shears
- Straightedge
- Fabric marker
- Pins
- Iron
- Sewing machine
- Fabric glue or self-adhering decals/sequins

1 To find straight grain of denim (important for the fringing), snip jeans near bottom hem and tear across. On the straight grain, cut 10¹/₂- by 5¹/₂-inch piece denim. Fold and press short ends ¹/₂ inch to right side.

2 Cut two 4¹/₂-inch pieces each ribbon and ball fringe. Fold short ends of each piece under ¹/₂ inch. Place ball fringe over both folded edges of the bag, centered about 1 inch from side edges. Stitch down center. Pin ribbon over ball fringe and stitch. Cut two 3-inch pieces ribbon. Form loops. (If the clasp set does not have a circle that can be opened, put the circular piece in ribbon loop before sewing loop.) Pin a ribbon loop at top of each side of bag, at an angle, and where it will be caught in the side seams. Fold bag so decorated edges come together and are on the outside. Stitch together sides of bag, 1 inch from edge.

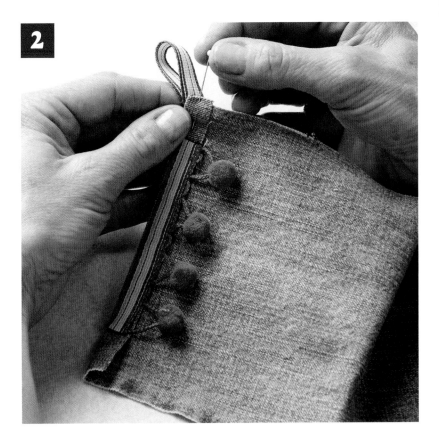

3 To make 8-inch strap, cut 10-inch piece ribbon (make strap longer if desired). Put end of ribbon through clasp, turn under ¹/₄ inch, make ¹/₂-inch loop, and pin. Stitch at folded edge. Repeat for other side. Attach circular piece to carrier loops, if not already done. Strap can be hooked to both sides of the bag, or at one corner. Using pin, fringe exposed seams by pulling each thread out up to the stitching. Glue on charms, decals, rhinestones, beads, or a decorative pin.

Message Board and Magnets

It is easy to turn an old painted metal tray into a colorful message board. Make a set of decorative magnets from small objects that reflect the theme of the tray. These glass pebbles look like the grapes painted on the tray.

$$

Materials

- Decorative metal tray
- 1 yard (¹/₈-inch) twisted cording
- ¹/₂-inch adhesive-backed magnetic strip
- Glass pebbles or other small decorative items

Tools

- Straightedge
- Masking tape
- Scrap wood
- Awl
- Hammer
- Scissors
- Denatured alcohol (optional)

1

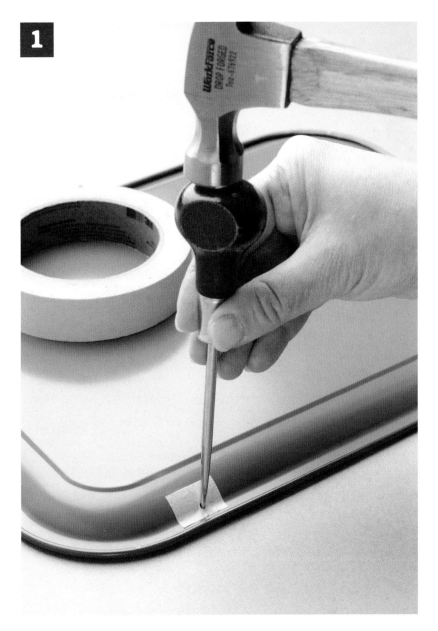

2

2 Tightly tape both ends of cord. Thread cording through holes in tray from back to front, twisting and jiggling the ends to get them through. Even up the ends of cording and tie in double knot several inches from end. Let the braid ravel decoratively to the knot.

3 Cut ¹/₂-inch pieces from magnetic strip. Trim off corners. Adhere each piece to back of a glass pebble and apply pressure. If backing does not stick, clean pebble first with denatured alcohol.

3

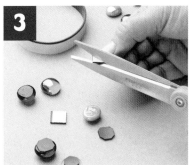

1 On back of tray, measure 3 inches from top corners and mark with masking tape. Place scrap wood under tray. Using awl and hammer, pound holes in tray from the back side. Turn tray over and pound down any sharp edges around holes.

Holiday Pouch Bag

This evening bag makes a fabulous gift. It is styled to match the Elegant Holiday Shawl (page 124). See the introduction to that project for tips on working with special-occasion fabrics. Choose fabrics such as taffeta, satin or silk. Avoid stretch fabrics.

$$

Materials

- 3/8 yard each of two special-occasion fabrics
- 5/8 yard medium-weight lining fabric
- 6-inch square plastic canvas
- Matching thread
- 3 yards satin cording

Tools

- Compass
- Straightedge
- Fabric marker
- Paper
- Scissors
- Rotary cutter and mat
- Pins
- Iron
- Sewing machine; zipper and buttonhole attachments
- Size 11 needle
- Tape measure
- Sewing needle
- Seam ripper

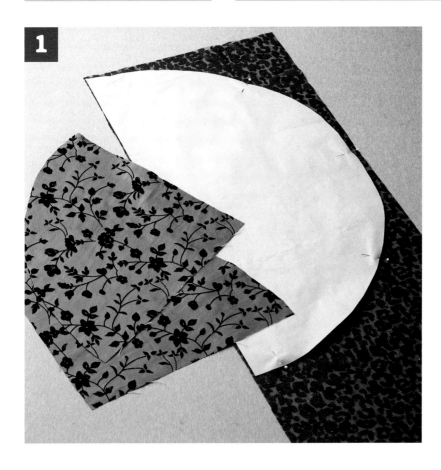

3 Pin the lining and the pieced fabric circles together, right sides together. Lining will be about 3/4 inch bigger. Stitch around circle about 1/2 inch from edge of pieced fabric circle, leaving 4-inch opening. Turn right side out and pin around edge. Be sure that seam is pulled out to edge. Do not press. Slipstitch opening closed.

4 Make 1/4-inch buttonholes along top of bag, 1/2 inch from edge. Space equally or approximately 4 inches apart. Using seam ripper, carefully cut buttonholes open.

5 Cut cording in half. Thread each piece through all buttonholes, passing in opposite directions. Pull together to form purse. Tie ends of cords together with an overhand knot.

1 Using compass and straightedge, make paper pattern for 22-inch-diameter circle. Use pattern to cut one half-circle of each special-occasion fabric. Fold each piece in half and cut, creating four pie-shaped pieces. Fold lining fabric in half, place straight edge of pattern on fold, pin and cut. Cut 4-inch circle of plastic canvas. Cut 5 1/2-inch circle of lining fabric.

2 Pin pie-shaped pieces together, alternating colors. Stitch. Press seams open gently. Hand stitch a long running stitch just inside edge of the small fabric circle. Place plastic circle over small fabric circle and pull stitching to wrap fabric around edges of plastic. Center wrapped plastic, fabric side down, over wrong side of pieced fabric circle and hand baste.

123

Elegant Holiday Shawl

A great addition to someone's little black holiday dress, you can make this beautiful wrap to match the Holiday Pouch Bag (page 122). A few tips on working with specialty fabrics: use a cool iron, press only gently and from the wrong side, pin only in the seam allowances to avoid holes, use a new needle, and finish seams with a serger or a zigzag stitch.

$$

Materials

- 1/3 yard flocked taffeta (fabric A)
- 1/3 yard textured specialty fabric (fabric B)
- 1/2 yard (60 inches wide) sheer fabric (fabric C)
- 2/3 yard (60 inches wide) satin, silk, or taffeta (fabric D)
- Matching thread
- Tube size 8 or 11 iridescent seed beads
- Beading thread
- Four larger beads (optional)

Tools

- Straightedge
- Rotary cutter and mat
- Scissors
- Pins
- Iron
- Sewing machine
- Size 11 needle
- Sewing needle
- Beading needle

1 Using straightedge, rotary cutter, and mat, cut two 5-by 19-inch pieces fabric A; two 4- by 19-inch pieces fabric B, two 3- by 19-inch pieces fabric C, two 9½- by 19-inch pieces fabric C for lining; and one 51- by 19-inch piece fabric D. **Tip:** When cutting sheer fabrics, hold them to the mat with tape.

2 Pin and stitch together a piece of fabric A, B, and (smaller) C. Repeat for other pieces. Finish seam allowances and press away from sheer fabric. Stitch each pieced group to an end of fabric D. Finish seams and press toward fabric A.

3 Fold one long edge of lining ½ inch, press, and stitch. (Photo shows lining of contrasting color for clarity.) Place lining over

one end of shawl, right sides together, and pin on outside edges. Stitch, leaving few inches open for turning. Repeat for opposite end.

4 Turn shawl right side out. Pin edges together. Slipstitch opening closed. On long edges, press and sew ¼-inch double hem.

5 With beading needle and knotted thread, stitch into one corner of shawl. Pick up about 3½ inches of beads and stitch back into corner, forming loop. Repeat on other corners. If desired, thread about 2 inches of beads and pick up a larger bead, then a small bead and thread back through all the beads starting with large bead. Stitch a few times into the corner fabric and knot. Repeat for remaining corners.

125

Handmade Greeting Cards Gift Pack

Make cards for various occasions (birthday, get well, sympathy) and a matching address book. Tie together with voile ribbon and add a book of stamps and a fancy pen. This is a thoughtful gift the recipient will appreciate all year long.

$

Materials

- Card stock (8½" x 11")
- Scrapbook paper
- Embellishments
- Envelopes
- Printed address pages and address label refills
- Two brads
- Border stickers
- Book of stamps
- Ink pen
- 1 yard voile ribbon

Tools

- Straightedge
- Pencil
- Scissors, regular and decorative-edge
- Paper edger (optional)
- ¼-inch punch
- Glue stick

3 Stack cards, address book, and stamps and tie together with voile ribbon. Insert ink pen under ribbon.

1 Measure envelope. Cut card stock to fit into the envelope when folded in half. Decorate each card using scrapbook paper and embellishments.

2 Cut two pieces of card stock to form a cover for the address pages. Punch holes and insert brads to hold book cover and address sheets together. Embellish cover with border stickers.

Death by Chocolate

If you have a friend who loves chocolate (and who doesn't?), assemble this quick, easy and fun gift.

Due to your association with me
you have been placed on trial.
Your history has been studied
and you have been found guilty.
The sentence has been declared.
You must eat and drink
all the contents in this cup
thus creating
"Death by Chocolate"

Materials

- White coffee mug
- Piece scrapbook paper, chocolate print
- Melting chocolate
- Three pretzel rods
- Plastic spoon
- Three mini marshmallows
- Four sucker bags
- 1½ yards white narrow voile ribbon
- Card stock, cream
- Chocolate candy bar
- Package hot cocoa mix
- Six chocolate candies
- Transparent wrap
- Rubber band

Tools

- Tape measure
- Straightedge
- Pencil
- Scissors
- Glue
- Microwave-safe bowl
- Microwave
- Spoon
- ¼-inch punch

1 Measure around the cup and top to bottom. Cut piece of scrapbook paper to fit. Glue paper to cup.

2 Place melting chocolate in bowl and microwave. Spoon chocolate over two-thirds of pretzel rods. Dip plastic spoon into chocolate and add marshmallows. Chill until firm.

3 Cut four 8-inch pieces ribbon. Place pretzels and spoon in bags and tie with ribbon. Print message on cream-colored card stock: "Due to your association with me, you have been placed on trial. Your history has been studied and you have been found guilty. The sentence has been declared. You must eat and drink all the contents in this cup thus creating Death by Chocolate." Trim card stock. Cut 3- by 4-inch piece chocolate-print scrapbook paper. Glue message on paper. Punch hole in one corner.

4 Place spoon, pretzels, candy, and hot chocolate in cup. Cover with transparent wrap and hold with rubber band. Using rest of ribbon, tie card to gift pack, then form bow.

Beaded Handle Reversible Tote

Easy to sew, fun to carry and reversible, this tote can hold anything from your knitting to important papers.

$$$

Materials

- ⅝ yard decorator fabric (fabric A)
- ⅝ yard contrasting decorator fabric (fabric B)
- ⅝ yard of fusible quilting fleece
- Four (¾-inch) D-rings
- 1 yard (16-gauge) wire
- 40 assorted wood beads

Tools

- Straightedge
- Fabric marker
- Scissors
- Iron
- Pins
- Sewing machine
- Thread
- Needle-nose pliers

1 Cut two 16- by 17-inch rectangles each of fabric A, fabric B, and fleece. Fuse fleece to wrong side of fabric A following manufacturer's instructions.

2 Place pieces of fabric A together, right sides together. Pin. Stitch sides and bottom with ½-inch seam allowance, pivoting at lower corners. Press seam allowances open. Repeat with pieces of fabric B.

3 To make bottom of tote, fold a bottom corner of fabric A 2 inches from the point. Mark line. Stitch across. Repeat on other side. Trim seams to ¼ inch. Repeat with fabric B.

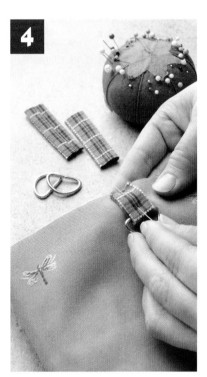

4 To make holders for the handles, cut 2- by 8-inch strip fabric B. Fold in half the long way with right sides together. Stitch ¼-inch seam. Turn right-side out. Press strip with seam centered in back of strip. Cut strip into four 2-inch pieces. Make each into a loop and place a D-ring in center. Pin each 2 inches from a side seam on the front and back of the bag. Baste.

5 Place the fabric A bag inside the fabric B bag with right sides together. Match side seams and top cut edges. Stitch with ½-inch seam, leaving a 6-inch opening at one side seam. Turn bag right side out and press upper edge. Slipstitch opening closed.

6 Cut two 15-inch pieces wire. Using pliers, bend up ¼ inch at one end. Thread wood beads to desired length. Bend wire end up and trim excess wire. Loop handle ends through D-ring and close with pliers. Repeat for other handle.

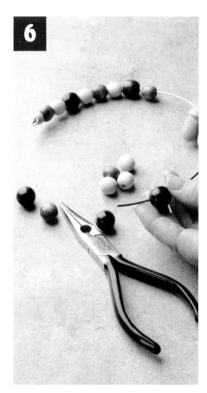

Chapter 5

Finishing Touches

Terrific Tags

Pleated, fringed or trimmed, this collection of gift tags offers up a creative way to use scraps and personalize presents.

To:

From:

to:

from:

$

Materials

- Card stock: white, pink, red, green, yellow, black, metallic gold, pink, turquoise
- Felt squares: light, medium, and dark green
- Scrapbook paper, green polka dots and checks
- Pom-poms: purple, red
- Scraps of jumbo yarn: turquoise, green, red, pink
- Alphabet stickers
- Old holiday greeting cards

Tools

- Compass
- Double-stick tape
- Decorative scissors, wavy edge
- Paper cutter
- Scissors
- Punches: 1/4-inch, star, 3/4-inch
- Black fine-tip marking pen
- Tracing paper
- Pencil
- Hot glue gun and glue stick
- Tape
- Eyelet tool and eyelets

1 To make pleated tree tag, using the compass, trace 2 3/4-inch-diameter circle on green card stock. Cut out. With double-stick tape, attach circle to white card stock. Cut wavy edge, then cut circle in half to make two trees. Fold each tree in half. Fold each edge to the fold line. Overlap the ends and tape to form dimensional tree. Cut tag from card stock Tape tree to tag.

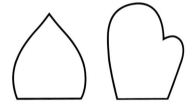

3 To make mitten or hat tag, enlarge pattern by 400% and cut out. Place on scrapbook paper and trace. Cut out. Tape to card stock. Trim with decorative-edge scissors. Punch hole at top. Thread yarns through hole and tie. Hot-glue a pom-pom over hole.

4 To make woven tag, cut card stock desired size. Cut 6 or more strips from card stock to fit within tag dimensions. Weave strips together. Tape in back. Trim woven piece to desired size.

Punch 3/4-inch hole in the weaving. Tape woven piece to a tag. Place sticker letter in hole. Insert eyelet in the tag.

2 To make four fringed tree tags, cut tags from card stock. Punch star-shaped holes in tag. Cut 1 1/2-inch circle of light green felt, 1 3/4-inch circle of medium green, 2 1/4-inch circle of dark green. Cut each circle in quarters. Fringe rounded edges. Overlap three pieces and tape to tag. Using pen, draw trunk and star.

5 To make recycled greeting-card tags, cut tag of desired size from card stock or greeting card. Cut or punch shapes from the greeting cards.

Heavenly Greetings

These sweet cherubs are accented with stars, sparkles and feathers. Rhinestone letters send an emphatic Christmas message.

Materials

- Decorative paper, star print in silver or blue
- 5- by 7-inch white blank cards with envelopes
- Card stock: silver, white, pink, purple, blue
- Double-stick tape
- Two white feathers
- Adhesive acrylic rhinestones, star and moon shapes
- Adhesive crystal letters

Tools

- Paper cutter or scissors
- Straightedge
- Pencil
- Punches, 3/4-inch and 1-inch
- Tracing paper

1

4a

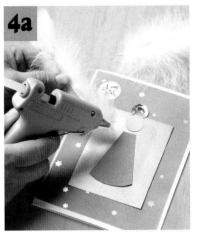

4b

1 Cut 4½- by 6½-inch piece print paper. Tape paper to the card. Holding paper vertically, punch 1-inch circle ¼ inch from upper left corner.

2 Cut 3- by 4-inch piece silver card stock. Tape 1 inch from the bottom of star paper and centered.

3 Trace gown pattern. Cut out. Place on purple or blue card stock and trace. Cut out. Tape gown ³/8 inch from bottom of card. Punch ³/4-inch circle from pink card stock. Tape ¹/8 inch above gown.

4 Press rhinestone star in white circle on card. Press a moon or a crystal letter "O" on the head to look like a halo. Hot-glue one feather on each side of gown, trimming ends as needed. Press a word onto white card stock. Trim, leaving a narrow border. Center and tape at bottom of card.

Poinsettia Gift Box

This box will hold your gift elegantly, and later can be used as a holiday decoration. You can create this easy project in less than an hour.

Materials

- Oval papier mâché box: 6½ inches wide by 9 inches long by 4½ inches high
- Two sheets holiday-print scrapbook paper
- 12-inch square gold metallic paper
- 26 inches of ¼-inch burgundy organdy ribbon
- 1 yard gold satin cording
- 12-inch square burgundy suede paper
- Medium glue dots
- Six ½-inch foam squares
- Gold liquid beads

Tools

- Paper trimmer or straightedge and scissors
- Glue
- Clear tacky glue
- Tacky glue
- Hot glue gun and glue stick
- Leaf-shape template
- Cutting tool
- Mat
- Palette knife or craft stick

3 Using template, mat, and cutter, cut 22 leaves from suede paper. Alternatively, draw a leaf pattern and cut leaf shapes with scissors.

4 Using tacky glue, glue seven leaves to center of lid. Continue layering leaves, placing foam squares under last six leaves. Using palette knife or craft stick, add beads in center of poinsettia.

1 Cut two 4½- by 12-inch strips print paper. Glue to outside of box. Cut two ¾- by 12-inch strips gold paper. Glue to sides of lid. Place top of lid on print paper and trace. Cut out. Glue to top of lid.

2 Using clear tacky glue, attach ribbon to outside edge of lid. Hot-glue satin cording around upper edge of lid.

Oatmeal Box Package

Present holiday cookies or candies in this festive package made from an empty oatmeal box. After Christmas, hang the box on a door to hold keys or mail.

Materials

- Empty small oatmeal box
- Kraft paper or plain grocery bag
- Green card stock
- Brown print paper
- Dimensional snow
- Gold liquid beads
- Matte dimensional paint, pistachio green
- 12 inches (18-gauge) copper wire
- 16 inches fluffy green trim

Tools

- Straightedge
- Pencil
- Scissors
- Tacky glue
- Christmas template
- Cutting tool
- Mat
- Toothpick
- Craft stick
- 1/4-inch hole punch
- Needle-nose pliers
- Hot glue gun and glue stick

1 Discard lid of oatmeal box. Cut 7- by 13-inch piece kraft paper. Glue to box. Allow to dry. Using template, cut Christmas tree from green card stock and trunk from brown print paper. (Alternatively, draw patterns and cut with scissors.) Glue trunk and tree to box.

2 Embellish tree with random dots of dimensional snow. Dip toothpick into liquid beads and apply random dots to tree. Apply dots of pistachio dimensional paint to tree. Allow to dry. Using craft stick, apply dimensional snow below tree trunk and around bottom of box. Allow to dry.

3 Using hole puncher, punch holes at opposite sides of box at the top. Insert ends of wire.

Using needle-nose pliers, bend ends of wire to secure handle. Hot-glue trim around top of box.

141

Cylindrical Gift Bags

With just a bit of math, you can make a tall-and-skinny gift bag in a custom size that perfectly presents what you're giving.

Materials

- Cotton fabric
- Matching thread
- Rickrack

Tools

- Compass
- Pencil
- Scissors
- Straightedge
- Calculator
- Sewing machine
- Pins

1 To make bottom of bag, place base of gift on wrong side of fabric. Lightly trace circle around gift. Using compass, round out the circle. Add 1/2-inch seam allowance. Cut fabric circle.

2 To make sides of bag, measure height of gift and add 2 or more inches depending on how much excess fabric you want at the top.

3 Determine width by measuring across fabric circle, multiplying by 3.14, and add 1

inch for seam allowances. Cut rectangle of fabric to this height and width. If you are using more than one fabric, piece the fabric together before cutting out rectangle. Fold rectangle in half lengthwise, right sides together, and sew together with 1/2-inch seam allowance. Sew double 1/2-inch hem at top.

4 Stitch 1/2 inch from edges of fabric circle. Clip to stitching line every 1/2

inch. With pins, mark fourths of circle and rectangle. Pin circle and rectangle together, right sides together, raw edges even, and matching pin marks. With bag facing up, stitch a 1/2-inch seam around the bottom of the bag. Turn right-side out. Tie rickrack around top to close bag.

Holly Leaves Card

Make your own greeting cards for Christmas. These cards are easy to make … and you can add sweet treats!

Materials

- Green card stock
- Candy print paper
- 4- by 5½-inch red card with envelope
- Three (½-inch) foam squares
- White paper
- Red liquid beads
- 12 inches white fluffy yarn
- Wrapped peppermint

Tools

- Paper cutter or straightedge and scissors
- Crimper
- Holly punch
- Glue
- Toothpick
- ¼-inch punch

1 Cut card stock: 4 by 6 inches, 1½ by 5½ inches, 1½ by 2½ inches. Cut candy print paper: 1 by 4¾ inches, 2 by 3¼ inches, 1 by 4⅜ inches. Crimp the middle-sized piece card stock. Glue crimped paper to left side of card. Using foam squares, attach smallest print paper to crimped paper.

2 Using computer, print "C-H-R-I-S-T-M-A-S" vertically, 4 inches top to bottom. Trim paper to ⅝ by 4⅜ inches. Glue the word to candy print strip. Punch holly leaves from green card stock, saving punched-out stock. Glue leaves on right side of card. Using toothpick, apply randomly a few liquid beads to holly leaves. Glue candy to base of word. Punch ¼-inch hole in upper left corner of card. Insert yarn and knot.

3 Using computer and white paper, print your Christmas greeting. Trim to 1¼ by 2¼ inches. Glue to 1½- by 2½- inch green card stock. Glue card stock to 2- by 3¼-inch candy print paper. Glue greeting to inside of card.

4 To make the envelope, glue 1- by 4⅜-inch candy print paper to left side of envelope. Trim the saved punched-out card stock to fit over candy print and glue. Check with your local postage service for any mailing stipulations in thickness of this card. Extra postage may be required.

Santa Box

This Santa will put a smile on anyone's face even before they open the box to find the gift.

$

Materials

- White box, 3 by 3 by 5 inches
- Acrylic craft paint, flesh color
- 3- by 5-inch piece white batting
- Two (1/2-inch) oval wiggly eyes
- Adult-size red sock
- Red thread
- White (2-inch) pom-pom
- 1 1/2- by 12-inch piece faux fur
- Sprig silk holly with berries

Tools

- 1-inch sponge brush
- Copy machine
- Pins
- Fabric marker
- Scissors
- Tacky glue
- Sewing needle
- Straightedge
- Hot glue gun and glue stick

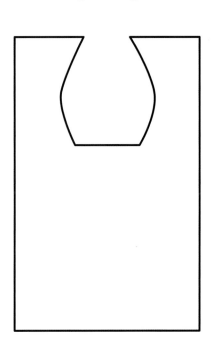

2 Enlarge pattern 150%. Cut. Pin pattern to batting and trace around. Cut out. Glue beard, moustache, and eyes to painted side of box.

3 To make hat, cut off top of sock. Using needle and thread, gather along edge. Hot-glue pom-pom to hat. Fit hat over top of box and turn up 1 inch. Hot-glue fur to hat band. Hot-glue holly to hat.

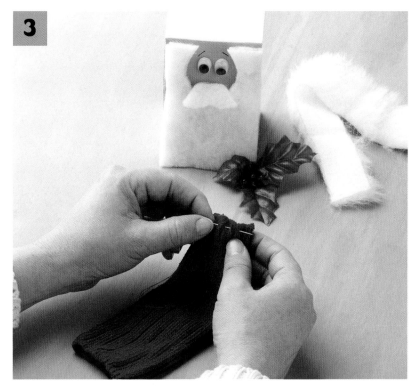

1 Paint one side of box. Allow to dry.

Picture-Perfect Greetings

Create photo greeting cards from bits of the cards you received last year.

Materials

- Envelope
- Card stock: red, green, white, or other
- Recycled holiday greeting cards
- Photograph

Tools

- Straightedge
- Pencil
- Paper cutter or scissors
- Circle punch
- Double-stick tape
- Decorative punch (optional)

3 Cut piece of card stock ½-inch larger than photo. Tape photo to card stock. Tape matted photo to front of card.

4 Punch or cut a small embellishment. Glue to flap of envelope.

1 Measure envelope. Cut and fold card stock to fit envelope.

2 Using photo for inspiration, cut or punch shapes, strips, or squares from old greeting cards. Arrange the shapes on the card front, keeping the size and shape of the photo in mind. Tape.

Felt Snowman
Gift Bag and Tag

Why purchase ho-hum gift bags when you can create this fun one in no time? Let it snow, let it snow, let it snow!

To: TOM
From: SUE

Gift tag snowman

1 To make tag, trace snowman pattern. Cut out. Place pattern on white card stock and trace. Cut out snowman. With marking pen, draw face, "To" and "From." Tie tiny ribbon bow and glue to chin. Punch hole in top of head and insert gold cording.

2 To make gift bag, enlarge snowman pattern 200%. Cut out. Place pattern on white felt and trace. Cut snowman and snow. Cut carrot nose from orange felt. Cut 1/2- by 6-inch piece red felt for scarf. Placing scarf under neck area, glue snowman 1 1/2 inches from bottom of gift bag. Cut 3/8-inch fringe on ends of scarf. Tie scarf and secure with glue to gift bag and snowman.

Materials

- White card stock
- 6 inches (1/8-inch) red satin ribbon
- 10 inches gold cording
- 8- by 10-inch blue paper gift bag
- Felt squares: red, orange
- 6- by 8-inches white felt
- Three evergreen-tree buttons
- Two (1/2-inch) red metallic pom-poms
- Five (1/4-inch) black buttons
- Two (1/4-inch) white buttons
- Three snowflake buttons

Tools

- Tracing paper
- Fine-tip marking pen
- Scissors
- Copy machine
- 1/8-inch punch
- Clear tacky glue

3 Glue snow at bottom of gift bag. Glue tree buttons along snow horizon. Glue pom-poms to each side of snowman for earmuffs. Glue nose and two black buttons onto face.

Nose

Gift bag snowman

Snow

4 Glue three black buttons onto body. Randomly glue snowflake buttons and white buttons in sky area. Tie tag to handle of bag.

Fabric Sew-On Card

$

Materials

- 8½- by 11-inch piece white card stock
- Green holiday print fabric
- Iron-on double-sided adhesive
- Matching thread
- Christmas greeting rubber stamp
- Pigment inkpad
- Gold embossing powder
- Iron-on ribbon, or ribbon and glue

Tools

- Straightedge
- Pencil
- Paper trimmer with scoring blade
- Tracing paper
- Scissors
- Iron
- Sewing machine
- Embossing heat gun

1 Using straightedge and pencil, mark along 11-inch edge of card stock at 1¹³/₁₆ inches, 1⁷/₈ inches, 3⁵/₈ inches, 1⁷/₈ inches and 1¹³/₁₆ inches. Using paper trimmer with scoring blade, score a line at each of these marks. Or, place ruler at each mark and score using a stylus. Fold along score lines.

2 Enlarge tree pattern 200%. Trace and cut out. Following manufacturer's instructions, adhere adhesive to back of fabric. Twice trace pattern on iron-on adhesive.

3 Cut tree halves and adhere to outer sections of card. Stitch around edges of each tree section.

4 Stamp greeting on center section of card. Sprinkle with embossing powder. Shake off extra powder and apply heat with heat gun to emboss greeting. Adhere or glue ribbon on outside sections of card, ½ inch from edge.

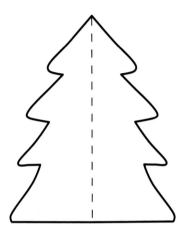

Pretty Packages

Make a quick greeting card, tag or place card with mosaic stickers and sparkly fibers. You will find braid with embroidery supplies wherever you shop for craft supplies.

$$

Materials

- Snowflake scrapbook paper
- 3½- by 5-inch blank white cards with envelopes or 1½- by 3¾-inch white place cards with silver border
- Mosaic sticker tiles, 1-inch and ⅜-inch
- 6-inch piece of braid
- Small silver or gold beads
- White thread
- Black fine-tip marking pen

Tools

- Straightedge
- Pencil
- Scissors
- Double-stick tape
- Large-eyed, sharp needle
- Sewing needle

1 To make a greeting card, cut 1½- by 3½-inch strip snowflake paper. Tape to front of greeting card, ⅝ inch from left edge of card. Press a tile to the right of the paper strip, centered left to right and slightly below the center top to bottom. To make a place card or gift tag, press a tile ⅜ inch from the left edge and ⅛ inch from bottom edge.

2 Using a sharp needle, poke a hole above center of tile. Poke holes ¼ inch to the left, right, and above first hole. Poke holes between the holes. Poke one hole centered below the tile.

3 Thread needle with braid and knot end. From back, bring needle through hole below tile. Pass braid over tile and insert needle in center hole on top. Stitch through each hole at top, returning to the center hole each time. Using sewing needle and white thread, sew a bead in center of bow. Using pen, write message or name. On envelope flap, press ⅜-inch tile on point.

Index

A

B

C

D